CELEBRATIONS

Also by Caterine Milinaire

Birth
Cheap Chic
Cheap Chic Update

Celebrations

TEXT BY CATERINE MILINAIRE

WITH CAROL TANNENHAUSER

PHOTOGRAPHS BY CATERINE MILINAIRE

DESIGNED BY JOAN PECKOLICK

HARMONY BOOKS/NEW YORK

Inquiries should be addressed to Harmony Books, a division of
Crown Publishers, Inc., One Park Avenue, New York,
New York 10016

Printed in Japan by Dai Nippon Printing Co. Ltd., Tokyo.

Published simultaneously in Canada by General Publishing
Company Limited

Library of Congress Cataloging in Publication Data

Milinaire, Caterine.
Celebrations.

Bibliography: p. 123
1. Festivals—Pictorial works. 2. Holidays—Pictorial works. I. Title.
GT3932.M47 1980   394.2   80-24535
ISBN 0-517-531062

10 9 8 7 6 5 4 3 2 1
First Edition

For Serafine and people who take celebrations a little further…

CONTENTS

INTRODUCTION

At first glance twentieth-century celebrations appear to be less important in our lives than they have been in the past. But even though the fast pace of the modern world has changed our perceptions and attitudes toward celebrations, they still remain integral to our lives—marking the family and seasonal passages that are part of the human experience.

On a taxi ride from Oakland to San Francisco several years ago, I had a conversation with the driver that emphasized my growing curiosity over the fate of modern day celebrations: Can the spirit be restored to our family and seasonal celebrations? Our conversation triggered a two-year quest that led me to the four corners of the world.

The taxi driver was curious about where I was headed with all of the camera equipment hanging from my shoulders. It was February 14, and I was on my way to photograph the events commemorating St. Valentine's Day, the official date on which people the world over celebrate love. In this particular instance the celebration was to take the form of a one-hundred-square-foot carrot cake baked for the lunchtime crowd pouring out of the office buildings in downtown San Francisco. All of this celebrating perpetuated the Roman festival of fertility centering around Valentinus (from the Latin *valens,* meaning strength).

The taxi driver could not believe that in this day and age such elaborate festivities could take place on February 14, and I wondered how he could avoid at least a knowledge of the event. When I asked him to name his favorite celebration, he seemed quite amazed by his own answer: "I don't celebrate anything." I proceeded to name all of the family and seasonal celebrations I could think of, but there was no celebratory occasion that marked his life, not even a birthday—either his mother did not remember or she had too many children to single out for cake and candles. My "uncelebrated" cab driver was now in his early forties and had never gotten married because it cost too much, and, besides, few people married anymore, at least not in his neighborhood. He had a child, but could not remember any welcoming rites being performed when the baby was born. His mother lived in another part of the United States and he had not seen her in a long time. His real immediate family were his friends. When anyone died, all he knew was that someone looked up the nearest crematorium in the Yellow Pages. He liked the idea of celebrating, but there was not much he could relate to—Christmas was a frenetic present-buying race; New Year's was just another day, usually spent in a bar drinking beer with friends; and most other holidays were government imposed, with little meaning to his life.

It was hard to believe that he did not celebrate at least one event once in a while. After a few moments of searching his memory, he came up with Thanksgiving. It always falls on a Thursday, he said, and on Friday you have to report back to work. The government sets it up as a special day, not part of a quick getaway weekend out of town. Thanksgiving, he began reminiscing fondly, was always spent around a table of unusually good food and in the company of many friends. While he recalled the gastronomical pleasures of this autumn celebration, I could not help but draw a parallel to my own way of dealing with the celebrations, rituals, and ceremonies engendered by my own family or decreed by society. For a long time after my childhood I did not want to be a part of any of it.

My childhood years had been filled with various sanctified rites of passage and seasonal rejoicings that occurred year in and year out with monotonous regularity. As I grew into adolescence, I began to intensely dislike all of the ceremonial trappings of church and state and the forced rituals that drained all spontaneity from these events, leaving me with nothing to do but endure the calcified gestures of the officiant. Today, as an adult in the middle of my life, I can better understand some of the reasons why I had been avoiding birthday parties, weddings, funerals, parades and picnics—the celebratory *spirit* was missing.

The taxi driver and I wished each other a happy St. Valentine's

Day as I got out of the car at the Embarcadero Center. Behind the huge heart-shaped carrot cake was a string quartet playing romantic music. Tall mime characters with white-painted faces waltzed with people from the lunchtime crowd. On the sidelines a young man exhibited a large red heart pinned to his lapel that said, "Kisses for $1." The crowd, mostly office workers of a similar age group, appeared to enjoy the break in their midday routine, but I felt that something was missing.

After photographing the dancing and the cutting of the enormous cake, I left for the Hall of Flowers where the Department of Parks and Recreation of the city of San Francisco was giving the Second Annual Senior Citizens' Valentine's Day Dance. A lively band provided the music for the older men and women, who were festively dressed and had bright red hearts prominently displayed. The surprise of the afternoon was a slender man dressed up as cupid. This overgrown angel jumped around shooting heart-shaped arrowheads at women who, when they returned them, got a huge kiss. But there was something missing in this celebration, too.

It was sunny in the park outside, and I went to sit on a nearby bench. I asked the woman next to me if she liked the dance. That they called her a senior citizen, she said, she couldn't do much about—that was their classification and nowadays everything had to be classified—but why did they restrict the dance to senior citizens? She did not understand why it couldn't have been for anyone wishing to share Valentine's Day with them.

The same type of compartmentalizing had bothered me at the cake event. Just as she had felt the lack of an extended family in her life, I was missing the likes of her in mine. Anyone can pray alone, fast alone, worship the sun or invoke the holy spirit in solitary splendor, but what of a wedding, Christmas, a funeral, where there are no grandparents, no young children, no mixing of the generations? Peer-group separation exists in daily activities, but family and seasonal festivities have always been occasions when the different generations could come together and share in the celebration. The mingling of people at a seasonal renewal or a family passage always generates excitement and a welcome break in the daily routine.

As our celebrations have lost their meaning, people have turned to other, more modern rituals: Storytelling around the campfire as a form of passing knowledge from older to younger generations has been replaced by television. Tribal dances, which traditionally included mating and trance dances, are faintly echoed in today's discoteques. More happens in parking lots these days than in public plazas. Masses of religious devotees are transformed in our electronic age into thousands of fans at a rock concert. The libation rite has become the daily cocktail hour. The olympiads are replayed on the football field every Monday night. Common causes for the advancement of civilization are promoted by street demonstrations, political conventions, or rallyings of the troops. Even getting in touch with the inner self has changed in the twentieth century: The coming-of-age ceremony has been replaced in most of the Western world by encounter groups, and the therapist has replaced the priest in his confessional.

Our celebrations have been diminished in strength because their original purpose has often been lost or forgotten or exploited by commercialism. The evolution of women in the past decades may have also contributed to the change in the nature of celebrations, which have been passed on in primarily matriarchal ways. People are attempting to revitalize their celebrations by understanding the origins of their traditional ceremonies and creating their own interpretations of age-old customs with rituals more befitting their lives.

In this book I have attempted to record the way we all celebrate rituals and ceremonies, from birth to death and from New Year's to Christmas. I have compiled a document, arranged in chronological order, of how groups and individuals around the world celebrate a particular passage of life, or change of season, in the hope that it will inspire people to see many more possibilities in their approaches to their important occasions. I have chronicled the ceremonies as a witness of my time, in a world quick to forget its past, for the children and adults of tomorrow.

Many Blessings
Caterine Milinaire

CELEBRATIONS

FAMILY CELEBRATIONS

These are the special occasions of the personal life cycle, experienced from birth to death. In today's fragmented world they are often the only times families come together, times when one or a few are honored, but the ties between all are renewed. They are private times, times to commemorate an important human passage, but also to measure the progress of the family, to share experiences and disappointments, to talk of the past and see how the children have grown. Most important, they are times when generations mingle; when the passing of knowledge from old to young is as natural as conversation; when the joy of an event is intensified, or the sorrow of it eased, because it is shared.

PREGNANCY

$\mathscr{F}$or this mother-to-be and her child, for all the members of their family and community, there will be countless celebrations, joyous and solemn occasions marking the changing of the seasons, the worship of a deity, the memory of a great person or event, and the momentous passages of human life. Few will compare in intensity of emotion to the celebration of the conception of life.

Joy, humility, wonder, and pride accompany the awareness of pregnancy. Friends and family congratulate the couple on their fruitfulness and toast the tiny being that is forming in its mother's womb. For the mother, it is a time of intense physical awareness and change, of excitement, fear and a strong sense of being "special." For the couple, it is a time of preparation, emotional and practical, for the great event that will soon profoundly change their lives. Pregnancy is a time of transition, perhaps the longest, quietest, most intimate passage. Highlighted by moments such as the first audible beat of the heart and the first nearly imperceptible flutter of movement, it is as close to magical as any human experience; nine months of wondrous growth and sweet suspense culminating in the miraculous moment of birth.

THE BIRTH OF MANUEL

A new life comes to Earth. A child is welcomed.
Moving and profound....Childbirth.

arie-Odile and Claude Layrisse, a French couple, chose to create their own quiet ceremony for the birth of their son. The setting was a small hospital near Paris. There, Dr. Michel Odent has transformed a space adjoining the traditional hospital delivery room into a cozy bedroom. With the security of knowing that, should she need them, the most modern medical facilities were only a door away, Marie-Odile labored on soft pillows, in homelike comfort, quietly concentrating on how best to help her baby come forth. Claude whispered encouragements and, in between contractions, cooled her with fresh water and soothed her with music and gentle back massages. From time to time, a hospital nurse looked in to check their progress or ask if they needed something. Otherwise, the environment was totally theirs. Peaceful and private was the celebration of the birth of Manuel.

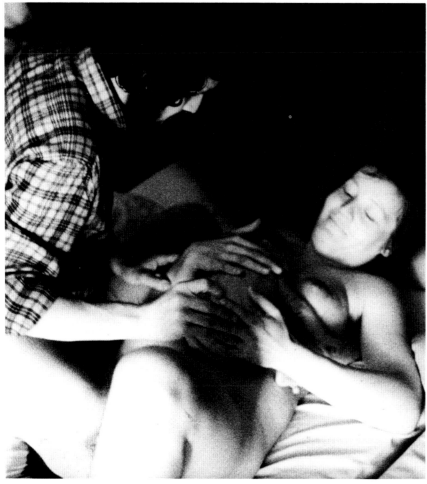

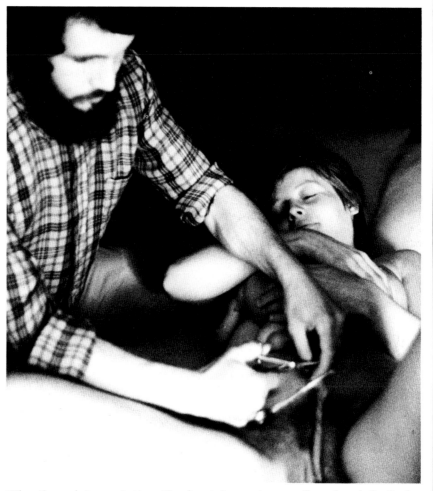

Joining hands, Marie-Odile and Claude hold and caress their baby, keeping him in a transitory semiembryonic position.

When the cord stops pulsating, Claude cuts it, severing actually and symbolically the baby's exclusive involvement with his mother.

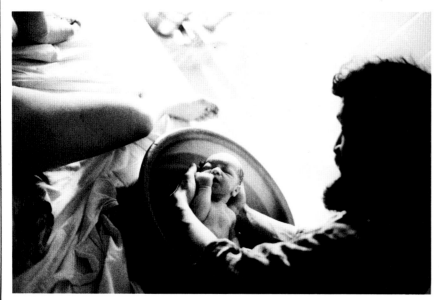

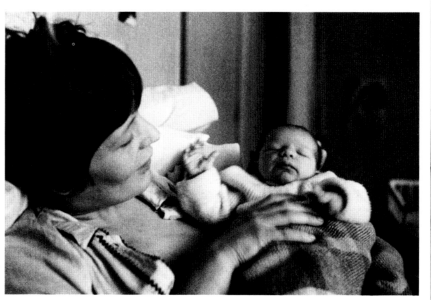

The initial baptism, a lukewarm bath, eases the transition from inside the womb to the outside world.

Snugly wrapped, baby Manuel enjoys his first meal at his mother's breast.

BABY'S DAY

t is the Sunday nearest the thirty-second day of life for a boy—or thirty-third day if the child is a girl—and so, as is the custom all over Japan, the baby is brought to the Shinto shrine for its first visit, called *Miyamairi*. Dressed in its finest clothes, the infant is held by its grandmother, a custom dating back to ancient times when new mothers were considered too impure to approach the god.

The family enters the temple grounds through a beautiful gate of cypress wood known as a *torii*. Sacred *sakari* trees bloom all around them as they make their way along the main walkway, bordered by stone lanterns donated by generations of worshipers. *Miyamairi* is the child's first encounter with people outside of the family, its first rite of passage into the society at large. At the shrine, everyone is purified by the priest, who waves a stick with hundreds of strips of white paper attached to one end above their heads. The waving of the *gohe* is meant to dispel any evil the baby may have brought with it from the other world. It gives the infant a clean and pure start in its present life, along with luck and blessings from the shrine's deities. The baby is then given a name with associations of good fortune.

After the ceremony, Baby's Day continues at the homes of friends and relatives where festive meals are served and gifts, toys, and good wishes are exchanged.

THE CHRISTENING
OF ANTONIO

G o, therefore Antonio, and make disciples of all nations, baptizing them in the name of the Father and the Son and the Holy Spirit…" (Matthew 28:19).

With those words, the family padre admitted the baby boy to the Christian faith, absolving him of Original Sin through the sacrament of baptism, transforming his mere human condition with the symbolic cleansing of water into that of an adopted child of God. At the same time Padre Achotegui christened him with the name Antonio, in honor of the saint, so that he might live inspired by that holy man and be recognized by others as a Christian.

Baptism is an ancient ritual with roots reaching back to early Jewish custom and, before that, to pagan rites of purification and incorporation into the community. Originally, baptisms were held in rivers. Today, most take place in church around the baptismal font, although some, like this Brazilian ceremony, are held at home. Elza and Carlos were named Antonio's godparents, guardians of his spiritual education should his parents die. It is Elza's honor to hold the baby, dressed in white to symbolize purity, throughout the baptismal ceremony. Carlos holds a lit candle signifying enlightenment by God's grace and acceptance by the Church. The padre begins to chant about the joy the birth has meant. He signs a cross on the child's forehead and bids the gathering of family and friends to repeat both gesture and prayers. The holy water is brought forth; Satan is renounced in a form of exorcism; and the blessed water is poured on Antonio's head, flowing into a large silver bowl that has been used for this purpose for generations. The tiny head is anointed with oil and the ceremony is complete.

Now it is the turn of Jacira Thome, the proud grandmother, to hold the newly baptized and christened Antonio.

THE MUNDAN OF INDRA

To the town of Varanasi, also known as Benares, on the banks of the Ganges River, the family of Indra has come. They have traveled far and saved for many years to make the journey to this most sacred of Indian towns, for Indra is five years old and ready to undergo the Mundan ritual.

The Mundan is a symbolic rite of passage centering on the ancient belief that hair started in the mother's womb will not grow strong unless it is cut. So, when an Indian child is one, three, or five years old, always beside a river, its head is completely shaved, except for one tiny spot called the *choti,* where Hindus say the center of nerves resides right above the brain. The *choti* is avoided for fear the scissors or razor will harm that vital spot, but also because of a lingering myth that says it is closest to the hand of God, there to grab should God wish to pull the child to the heavens.

After sunrise, as the officiating *pandhit* watches from beneath one of the many straw parasols that line the river banks, Indra's head is shaved, just as the heads of all Hindu boys and some girls have been shaved for centuries. He is then blessed by the *pandhit,* who draws a swastika—an ancient symbol of luck in the East—upon his head with wet clay. A red dot, called a *telak,* is applied to the forehead between his eyes honoring spiritual vision, the third eye. A bit of rice is added to the *telak* for prosperity. Then the boy and priest join together in a *puja* (devotion) to Ganesh, the round-bellied elephant deity invoked to remove all obstacles from Indra's path through life.

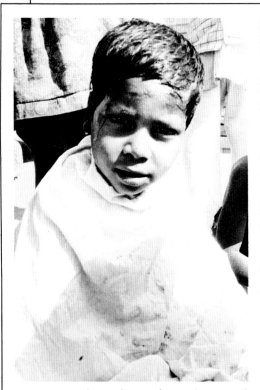

Looking to his family for comfort, Indra patiently waits to have his head shaved.

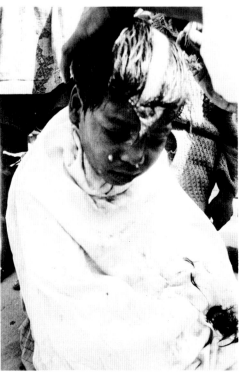

During the Mundan there is chanting in the air, incense burning, and sacred cows wandering.

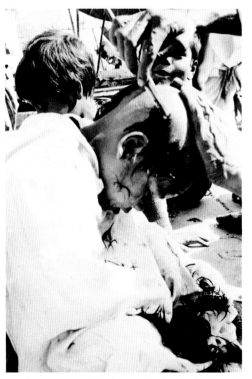

The long razor blade bares the child's skull to the morning breeze.

Holding flower offerings, Indra listens to the priests' incantations and blessings.

THE INITIATION OF JUAN CARLOS

Seven-year-old Juan Carlos lives in Brazil, two hours north of Rio de Janeiro. His family belongs to the Mãe da Serra Angola congregation of the Candomble cult, one of Brazil's oldest and most popular religions. Because Juan Carlos has displayed great interest and aptitude in spiritual matters, his parents have asked that he be initiated by the cult's leading priestess into the more subtle notions of mediumship. The purpose of the initiation is to develop his powers of communication with the spiritual realm.

What goes on in the small room where the *iawo* (initiate) retreats alone for twenty-one days before confirmation remains, for the most part, the congregation's secret. We do know that the ritual involves a symbolic death and rebirth. Juan Carlos must go through several days of prayers, fasting, and feats of endurance, some involving sacrificial animals. Even then, he can only join in the night of ritual celebration if one of the deities called upon manifests itself during his retreat.

Juan Carlos was incorporated by Iemanja, the goddess of the sea. Accordingly, he wears the white robe and pale blue sash representative of her devotees. His head is shaved except for a small round tuft at the top, and he wears a headband, armband, and necklace made of raffia straw to ward off any evil spirits.

The re-emergence of the *iawo* is celebrated by the entire congregation in an intense night of drumming, singing, and trance dances that last until dawn. Before parting, a communal meal is prepared using some of the animals sacrificed in the initiation ritual. After a few days, exhausted and quiet—inevitably changed—Juan Carlos returns to his family.

Disoriented, Juan Carlos emerges from the long retreat, gently guided by the Mãe de Santos.

In the center of the congregation Juan Carlos sways to the rhythm of the drums.

The initiates and priestesses pause as they move toward the drummers.

Juan Carlos bows to the power of the goddess Iemanja, his spiritual guide.

GIRLS' DAY

Hina Matsuri, Dolls' Festival, is celebrated in Japan on the third day of the third month of every year. Also called Girls' Day and the Peach Blossom Festival, it is a time for little girls to dress up, play hostess to their friends, pay homage to their ancestors, and be honored by their families. Fifteen antique dolls, dressed in their finest medieval clothes, are displayed in every home. Originally, the dolls had practical purposes: Nigno, for example, was an image carefully fashioned to protect against sickness; other, roughly made paper dolls were thrown into rivers to get rid of ill fortune.

BOYS' DAY

n the fifth day of the fifth month of the year, colorful carp fish streamers fill the skies of Japan, dancing and fighting the wind. The occasion is Boys' Day. The streamers symbolize the hope of families that their boys, like the strong carp fish who swims upstream, will be able to overcome the obstacles of life. Miniature symbols of bravery, such as swords and armor, are placed on the family altar. Games and customs display and echo the theme of strength.

CHILDREN'S DAY

The beginning of spring holds special meaning for the children of Katmandu, Nepal. Ghoda Jatra, the three-day horse festival, is celebrated and one of the days is set aside in their honor—Maru Satal, Children's Day, the festival of the Newar people.

Every year the children of Katmandu are told of the time the great god Mahadev assumed the form of an evil spirit and ate foods not usually consumed—meat, spirits, and garlic. Each district of the town holds a public meal to feed and honor its young.

The children are taken at dawn to the temple sanctuary to perform devotions and be blessed. Along with them go animals, contributed by local farmers, which are sacrificed, sanctified, and prepared by local women into nearly one hundred different dishes. The children line the streets, waiting patiently for their elders to serve them, while a group of merry musicians lends its notes to the celebration.

Later in the day a horse show will be presented for the royal family—a grand display of military equestrianism, pony relays, horse racing, gymnastics, helicopter bridge lifting, and motorcycle agility. In the evening families will feast on the meat of animals sacrificed earlier at the temple of the goddess Kali. Tomorrow will bring more visits to the temples of the main deities, after which symbolic representations of them will be paraded through town on splendid wooden palanquins, heralded by bands of merry musicians sounding drums, cymbals, and clarinets.

The king's household cavalry displays its equestrian talents in front of foreign dignitaries and the people of Katmandu.

The male head of the twenty-one-member family anoints the stone with red powder and oil and places morsels of food in the ground.

In the temple yard, animals are sacrificed to Kali and other demanding deities. Their meat will be used in the evening meal.

Grace is offered before the special meal of broiled buffalo and other meats seasoned with garlic, flat breads, beans, and rice.

At dawn the children dig out the "Luku Mahadyo," or hidden god, represented by a lingam stone, emblem of the god Shiva. At night the family gathers around it.

After everyone is served the women who have cooked the meal sit down to enjoy the special foods.

PUBERTY

       hirley Sago looked very solemn as she stood outside the ceremonial tepee, awaiting her meeting with the shaman. She was wearing a buckskin dress dyed the same yellow color as the sacred pollen that had been powdered on her face as a symbol of fertility and strength. Soon she would experience one of the most momentous occasions in the life of a Mescalero Apache woman—the puberty ritual, observed each year during the four-day Fourth of July celebration.

The Apache preparations for womanhood, the same for generations, are a well-guarded secret. Those who say they know the Apache ways tell of knots of hide the maiden must wear during menstruation; of sacred pollen being pinched from the bag hanging from Shirley's wrist to mark mothers and infants; of dancing; and of stretching face down on buckskins inside the tepee to be massaged by attendants while every part of the body is blessed for strength. One thing is certain, the deep chanting of the shaman and the sound of rattling deer hooves will be imprinted on the young woman's consciousness, evoking, for the rest of her life, the time she became a woman.

Shirley's rite of passage takes place on an ancient meeting ground. A brand new grandstand, numerous food concessions, and an arena alive with rodeo action give the area the look of a stadium. In the evening grand meals are cooked in the small round huts made of oak branches which have been especially built for the occasion. There is constant movement between the huts, tepees, trailers, and small campfires that dot the area, for the Fourth of July celebration is also a yearly reunion.

Later, around a colossal fire, the night's festivities continue with the mysterious Mountain Spirit Dancers.

THE MOUNTAIN SPIRIT DANCERS

*T*he Gan, or Mountain Spirit Dancers, are an intrinsic part of the Mescalero Apache puberty ceremonial. Outsiders often mistakenly refer to them as "devil" or "crown" dancers but, on the contrary, their role on each of the four nights is to bless the crowd and drive away any evil spirits that might disrupt the ceremony. The spirits they impersonate are identified by the specific mountaintops and caves that they inhabit. Every year the faces behind the black masks change, and often the identities of the dancers are unknown, even to tribe members. This year two young boys danced along with the grown men, learning the traditional ways but also breaking away from time to time into their own private rhythms. The jingling of bells on the dancers' waists and the crackling of logs on the fire gave a surrealistic feeling to the sight—a dimension of the beyond to the Mountain Spirit Dancers.

THE BAR MITZVAH
OF JONATHAN

One snowy morning in New Jersey, Jonathan woke up much earlier than usual and dressed carefully in a three-piece suit. As he knotted his tie in the mirror, he silently repeated the speech he had written to thank his parents and teachers for making this day possible. It was the day he was to publicly acknowledge the passing of his childhood and his acceptance of the spiritual responsibilities of a Jewish man. It was the day he would be recognized as a Bar Mitzvah—Son of the Commandment—in his coming-of-age ceremony.

Held on the Sabbath after his thirteenth birthday, Jonathan's Bar Mitzvah was preceded by years of study—Sunday school to learn the history and customs of his religion and Hebrew school to learn its language. Jonathan had spent many hours practicing his *haftorah,* the passage from the Book of Prophets he would read before the congregation of his family's Reform synagogue.

. The benches of the synagogue were filled with family and friends. Wearing the new prayer shawl, or *tallis,* his father had given him, Jonathan sat on the stage with another young man and a young woman who would share the ceremony with him. The coming-of-age ceremony of a Jewish girl is known as a Bat Mitzvah.

The service began with the cantor's call to prayer. The large Torah scrolls were solemnly removed from the ark and unrolled on the reading table. When Jonathan was called to read there was no hesitation in his voice. The Hebrew verses rang out clearly in the hushed house of worship. In turn, the rabbi blessed the new members of the religious community, called for a prayer in remembrance of the dead, and spoke to the young people with a mixture of wisdom and humor. Then the parents of the youths joined their children on the stage to be blessed and, in a moment of silence, to renew their own ties to the holy scripture.

Standing in front of the ark, the youths and their families contemplate their heritage and are blessed by the rabbi.

Jonathan's guests enjoy a sumptuous buffet, which begins with the blessing of the traditional challah bread.

In the front row Jonathan's parents listen to their son's haftorah *with a mixture of nervousness and pride.*

As Jonathan cuts his thirteenth birthday cake with an antique silver knife, his grandmother reaches for a kiss.

Back home, Jonathan takes off his tie and jacket and receives the congratulations of family and friends.

Traditionally, a candlelighting ceremony precedes the cutting of the magnificent Bar Mitzvah cake.

GRADUATION

You think it will never come, then one day you turn around and it's here—you're having your senior picture taken and picking up your cap and gown and wondering what tomorrow will bring. Although it may not appear so, it is certain that these students are feeling the importance of their graduation day: the pride of accomplishment after years of study, the fears and hopes for the future, the sadness of saying good-bye.

At Occidental College in California the families and friends of the graduates gathered in the Renisen Bird Amphitheater for an evening of pomp and circumstance. A brass band played as the members of the academic hierarchy took their assigned positions. An opening invocation by the college chaplain was followed by remarks and addresses by the deans and trustees and then, most awaited of all, the conferring of degrees. To the steady, rhythmic beat of the roll call, the students filed slowly by to receive their diplomas. There was a feeling of dignity, despite the occasional pranks and the political slogans sewn to the traditional black robes and mortarboards. As each name was called, applause sprang from the happy crowd. Then all bowed their heads for the final benediction and joined together in the singing of the alma mater.

THE BRIDAL SHOWER OF BERYL

The traditional bridal shower replaced the ancient custom of sending household presents to the bride-to-be upon the official announcement of her betrothal. Today, bridal showers are still a Western tradition, while engagement parties are a rapidly disappearing custom. The friends and family of Beryl chose to honor the ancient custom when, one Saturday afternoon, they surprised her at her home in Queens, New York.

Beryl's amazed expression triggered a roar of delight from the women who had gathered to greet her on her return from the market. Even her grandmother, who rarely leaves her house, was there. They had brought with them many gifts to help Beryl begin her married life in Nigeria, where her husband-to-be is from and where they would return to live. Beryl was delighted with the pots and pans, silverware, linens, and revealing negligees. Gaily she modeled the traditional bonnet made by her aunt from the ribbons and bows on the packages and the symbolic paper umbrella that had hung above the home-cooked buffet.

Beryl and her grandmother preside over a table laden with bridal-shower gifts. Beryl's family and friends provided many of the household goods that will help begin her new married life in Nigeria.

As a symbol of good luck, the bride-to-be wears a hat fashioned from the ribbons and bows that decorated the packages.

THE WEDDING OF GITA AND ASHOK

*A*lthough twenty-one-year-old Gita was born in Toronto and educated in London, she chose to be married in India, the land of her ancestors. In her words, "Of all the weddings I've witnessed around the world, none is as ceremonial as the Hindu."

The marriage of Gita and Ashok was arranged by their families, as many marriages still are in India. Although the custom of giving a dowry was outlawed several years ago, upon their betrothal Gita's family delivered 101 kilos of sweets, eleven baskets of fruit, and a number of gold bars to Ashok's family as a traditional gesture.

Gita was massaged daily for a month before the wedding. In the final few days she was kept separate from Ashok as relatives and friends poured into town. The day before the marriage the women of Gita's family gathered at her home for the *Mehndi* ritual—the applying of henna in intricate designs to the palms and feet as an omen of good luck. The *Mehndi* is performed by country women who travel from wedding to wedding solely for that purpose.

Later that day the bride's brothers and father presented her mother with several ornate saris to thank her for caring so well for her husband. The fact that he is still alive is to her credit, just as his death would be held against her.

On the morning of the wedding Gita was given a complete skin cleansing with herbs and wholemeal flour. After a purification ritual by the family priest, she was anointed with sweet-smelling oils, showered with gifts, and richly clothed and adorned. Later Ashok will give her one last ornament—the *mangel sutra,* a golden neck chain with small black beads, symbolic of marriage in the East, as the ring is in the West.

That night the two families will meet at last for the final, elaborate ceremony.

After two days apart from his bride-to-be, the groom, accompanied by his family, sets out on a decorated white horse to meet her.

It is a dazzling procession with music, dancers, and fireworks. One-third of the way, Ashok exchanges his mount for a white car.

The car is abandoned for a massive elephant that carries Ashok to where his bride and her family are waiting.

The father of the groom greets the bride's father by lifting him in the air.

Gita looks beautiful in a traditional heavy, gold-embroidered red sari.

The bride and groom greet each other with flowers. Children toss petals at them and elders tuck money into their garments.

Amid the pandhit's chanting of hymns and Vedic mantras, the couple perform parikrama, *the seven symbolic walks around the holy fire.*

In the Sindoordaan *ritual, Ashok applies vermilion powder to Gita's hair parting. She is veiled to emphasize her status as a wife.*

THE WEDDING OF LEILA AND YOUSSEF

One balmy spring night in Cairo, Egypt, Leila and Youssef were married in the Christian Coptic tradition in the church where her parents had been wed. Although it was a solemn occasion, the gathering of family and friends could not help smiling at the obvious love and warmth that emanated from the couple. As the ceremony began Leila's young niece giggled excitedly, impatient to throw the rose petals in her basket at the bride.

After a short service in which Leila and Youssef touchingly pledged themselves to each other, a choir burst into a deep Christian Orthodox chant accompanied by the rich tones of an organ. At the end of the ceremony Youssef was wrapped in a golden cape by a church attendant. As the priest blessed the couple one final time, he bestowed on each of them a golden crown. Rose petals glided gently down on the ecstatic bride as the newlyweds left the church in a gaily decorated car for the reception.

THE WEDDING OF AMIT AND RON

One late summer afternoon Amit and Ron were married in the Jewish tradition at the Connecticut home of her parents. Both live in Israel, but Amit wanted the intimacy of a family wedding in the familiar surroundings of her childhood. The couple fasted for an entire day before the ceremony, which was held outdoors to symbolize the hope that their descendants would be as abundant as the stars. Even a light drizzle could not mar their excitement as they toasted each other in front of the tent.

Under the *huppah,* or canopy, fashioned from a *tallit* (prayer shawl), the rabbi performed the traditional service of hymns, prayers, and blessings, then pronounced Ron and Amit man and wife. They sipped wine from the same glass and Ron slipped a band of unbroken gold on Amit's finger. "Behold you are consecrated to me with this ring according to the laws of Moses and Israel," he declared, and shattered a glass with his foot. Cries of *"Mazel tov!"*—"Good luck!"—sprang from the happy crowd.

THE WEDDING OF KIMURA AND ISACHIKA

The wedding of Kimura was elaborately planned, for she is of a traditional Japanese family that wanted to see her married in the finest manner possible. Twenty-six members of the family gathered at the Meiji temple in Tokyo for the wedding ceremony. As is the custom, Kimura's grandmother carried a photograph of her deceased husband, signifying his spiritual presence there.

Earlier, Isachika, the groom, had walked slowly through the temple yard, awkward in the traditional, long pant-skirt he wore. Kimura was radiant in three elegant *kimonos* worn in layers, the top one made of silk crepe decorated with flowers and birds of auspicious wedding significance. In her large *obi* belt, Kimura had tucked a mirror case and fan. On her head was a *tsunokakushi*, a hat designed to hide the horns that grow on jealous wives.

The officiating priest stood beside a scroll representing the deities Izahagi and Izanami, the first married couple in Japanese history. Next to him, on a low table, was a lacquer tray with a delicate arrangement of pine, plum, and bamboo branches symbolizing long life and success. Kimura and Isachika exchanged formal vows, then toasted each other with saki (rice wine). Later there was a lavish reception and dinner in the ballroom of a grand hotel.

THE WEDDING OF CARMEN AND JUAN

From the time she was a little girl, Carmen knew that on the day of her wedding she would wear a long, white lace gown and net veil reminiscent of the Virgin Mary. Her gown had been made for her in her home in Oaxaca, Mexico, which had been transformed by the wedding preparations.

When the morning arrived, Carmen was nervous—the bridal bouquet could not be found in her sister's bedroom, which had become a showcase for the flowers and presents sent by family and friends. It was late afternoon before everyone finally gathered for the family photograph before leaving for the Guadalupe Church.

Inside the church, Juan kept glancing anxiously at the large wooden doors. Stiff in his new suit, he was also nervous, convinced that Carmen had forgotten to watch the time. Two violinists played gaily as the crowd laughed and chattered in the pews.

Suddenly there was a commotion at the door. The organ struck a dramatic tone as Carmen entered, radiant on her father's arm. She bowed her head as Juan came to meet them and lead her to the altar. The gold-leafed baroque altarpiece, lit by hundreds of candles, shimmered before them. As they knelt on a red velvet cushion, the priest encircled both their hands with a rosary.

In the Catholic religion marriage is a sacrament reflecting Christ's own union with the Church. The couple performs the sacrament mutually, with all others serving as the Church's witnesses. Carmen and Juan were obviously awed by the splendor and importance of the moment as they each whispered "Si" to the priest's all-important question.

As they ran back down the aisle and out of the church, they were showered with rice, for luck, by their guests and attendants.

THE WEDDING OF KATHLEEN AND MICHAEL

Outside a little wooden wedding chapel sandwiched between a gambling casino and a souvenir shop, Kathleen and Michael waited to be married. The idea of a wedding in exotic, exciting Las Vegas seized them only a few days before, and with a few friends in tow, they had arrived in Las Vegas that morning from the quiet of Anaheim, California, for a weekend of vows and celebration.

They reserved a chapel for 5:00 P.M., not realizing that that hour is a prime time for Las Vegas weddings. A crowd of other couples with their families and friends stood outside the chapel, anxiously awaiting their turn.

Kathleen and Michael were paged to the inner sanctum by a dignified voice over a discreetly hidden loudspeaker. Since they came complete with their own witnesses, all Michael had to worry about was the ring—which he fiddled with all the way down the aisle, making sure every step of the way that it was still secure in his front pocket.

Ten minutes later, newly wed, the couple stepped back into the neon-lit evening, kissed and laughed and accepted the congratulations of friends.

THE WEDDING OF
TAWN AND HOWARD

he guests had arrived on time—Tawn's teen-age daughter and Howard's two children—but the couple was nowhere in sight. As friends and family stepped from the chilly New York air into the imposing downtown courtroom, the clerk kept asking if this was the bride- or bridegroom-to-be. Finally, Howard arrived with his mother, both impeccably dressed in fine wool suits. Noting Tawn's absence, he joked that maybe she had had a change of heart since breakfast. After all, marriage hadn't worked for either of them the first time. Their collective children booed.

When Tawn did arrive there was no longer any doubt about who was the bride. She looked magnificent in a dress and hat designed especially for the occasion. Two elevators carried the party to the judge's chamber. While he donned his black robe, friends snapped pictures of the couple and their families in his secretary's office.

The judge faced them across a huge wooden desk, an imposing, fatherly figure who performed the familiar service in a deep, firm voice. Howard almost forgot to say "I do." Tawn was so overcome with emotion, she hid her face in her hands. Pronounced man and wife, they had no trouble at all with the traditional kiss, which drew applause from the gathering. Next it was the judge's turn to kiss the bride; then out came the rice and off they all went for a festive champagne brunch.

That night there was a lavish party for family and friends.

MOTHER'S DAY

"Wear a red carnation for your mother."

The cynics among us who think Mother's Day was invented by florists and card companies might be surprised to learn that the custom of honoring mothers in the early spring dates back to antiquity. According to mythology, a yearly spring festival was dedicated to Rhea, mother of the gods Jupiter, Pluto and Neptune, and the goddesses Verta, Ceres and Juno. Early Christians set aside the fourth Sunday after Easter to honor Mary, the mother of Christ, and the English have been observing "Mothering Sunday" on the fourth Sunday of Lent.

In America, Mother's Day was officially created in 1914 when Woodrow Wilson proclaimed the second Sunday in May as "a public expression of our love and reverence for the mothers of our country." Actually, credit for the holiday should go to Anna M. Jarvis, a spinster and devoted daughter who, in the early 1900s, waged a one-woman campaign for a day honoring mothers. On May 9, the anniversary of her mother's death, she requested a special church service at which carnations—Mrs. Jarvis's favorite flower—were given out. From this came the custom of wearing red carnations to symbolize living mothers, and white ones for those who have died.

The idea of Mother's Day caught on rapidly and was inevitably commercialized. Advertisements stressed giving gifts and candy and sending flowers, telegrams and cards. So embittered was Miss Jarvis by this turn of events that she shut herself off from the world. She died penniless, blind and alone in a sanitarium in 1944.

FATHER'S DAY

"Wear a white rose for your father."

Thousands of years ago it was the custom in certain countries to set aside a few days to "appease the souls of fathers" through various graveside rituals and commemorative gatherings. Today, in America, there is a special day to "honor thy father"—every third Sunday in June is Father's Day. Some sons and daughters unfortunately must still travel to cemeteries, but luckier ones join with their fathers and families for festive meals and gift-giving. As on Mother's Day, commercial pressure is a strong incentive but so is the kind of quality fathering that exists today, perhaps as a result of changing parental roles and the smaller size of families.

BIRTHDAY

I n the realm of personal holidays there are few more universal or joyous than birthday celebrations. How enthralled are the eyes of a child as he gazes at the flickering candles on his decorated birthday cake. And how astonished is the face of a person who stumbles into her own surprise party. Gaily-wrapped presents, friends and families gathered together, the traditional singing along with the entrance of the cake—these are some of the customs that make birthdays special. Although at times we may resent the haste with which they come, there is still no better excuse for a party.

HOME/HOSPITALITY

To receive well is an art that requires a great deal of feeling as well as a certain amount of experience and ritual. People who enjoy and take pride in entertaining can turn the simplest visit into a celebration of friendship and hospitality.

The masters of hospitality and welcoming rituals may well be the Japanese, whose elaborate tea ceremony is part of their religious discipline. Less formal, but just as gracious, is the hospitality extended by this Egyptian man.

When Fouad entertains guests at his home near Cairo, they are not likely to forget it. In the sunny courtyard next to the house he unrolls a plush, vibrant handmade carpet and spreads it with soft pillows. On it he places a specially baked cake served with steaming-hot fresh mint tea. Then, while his guests enjoy the setting and sweets, Fouad disappears into a nearby open chamber to delight their ears with his skillful violin playing.

THE PASSING OF KNOWLEDGE

"You pace yourself so you do not exhaust yourself straight away, my son."

One of the most unfortunate failings of Western society is the segregation of old and young. As a result, knowledge that is naturally passed from one generation to the next in other societies often does not make the transition in the West. An exception is in the Icarilla Apache Indian tribe. Every year, during a three-day festival, they stage a symbolic passing-of-knowledge ritual.

The old man and young boy are walking in the preliminary parade of the Icarilla Apache foot race, the highlight of spirited competition between two camps within the tribe. It is during this show of endurance and available male strength that the symbolic passing of knowledge occurs. Before the race the medicine man blesses the participants and, in secrecy, smears them with fresh clay under the cover of a temporary hut. He then encourages the young to give the very best of themselves by whipping them lightly with aspen branches. As they approach the starting line, the old man, who has run the race many times before, offers some final advice to the boy.

THE "EASY FUNERAL" OF DENNIS HOPPER

"No digging if you can dig it," or *"fantasizing on self-disposal."*

I t all depends where I am when I die, of course, but if it is anywhere near the Taos community of American Indians, they have a custom for disposing of bodies that I'd like to follow. You see, Taos is the meeting ground next to the sacred mountains. When I die they'll wrap my body in a blanket. The color and design of the blanket will depend on the stature I've achieved in the community. A solid red one is really tough to get, but, between you and me, I figure I'll get it since I am an egomaniac.

"An old woman will direct the arrangement. She's spent her days giving life and raising children; now she presides over death. She and the eagle Kivamen—I'm not sure how many, it all depends on your lifetime contribution to society—they carry your body first to the Kiva to be blessed, then up the sacred mountains to the sacred lake. They lay it on the ground next to the path, which is constantly guarded from below. The old woman has an eagle feather which she points in the air in the four different directions, then places inside the blanket with the body. The body is then left to be absorbed by the elements. The animals may come and get it. Anyway, it gradually decomposes in the open air. The idea is that you return yourself to the earth and your strength, in turn, feeds it. You see, the American Indian knows that he is the rock, he is the water, he is the animal, he is the vegetation, he is everything that is not man-made. What is man-made, he knows he made."

I Gusti Lempad lived peacefully in the midst of his large family. He spent his last days drawing and painting the spirits around him before he quietly passed away at the age of one hundred and sixteen.

THE CREMATION OF I GUSTI LEMPAD

In his youth, in the village of Taman, near the town of Ubud in Bali, I Gusti Njoman Lempad had been told that if he wanted to live a long life he should not bother to learn to read or write, but follow his artistic calling. The advice was obviously good for this talented painter, for it was not until he was 116 years old that he began making provisions for his funeral.

He valued the simple things, he said. He did not want a grand funeral that would ruin his family financially and go against the way he lived. He added that he would be overseeing the details of a six-tiered cremation from the spirit world. Not long after, he died in his sleep.

Cremations in Bali are very public and joyous affairs. Once the first night wake has been performed, along with the exorcisms to ward off malicious spirits, the body is washed and then wrapped in embalming sheets and everyone helps decorate its symbolic last abode. A week or two later last rites are performed to ensure the safe departure of the soul from the body, and the procession to the funeral pyre begins.

Palm offerings, beautiful fabrics, flowers, and good-omen designs accumulate around Lempad's funeral bier.

The artisans of the village started sculpting the bull sarcophagus on the day Lempad died.

The village healer ensures the complete detachment of the soul from the body.

The body is placed on the bull and, after a procession and last blessings, the funeral pyre is set ablaze.

The painter's son looks on as the guests arrive at the funeral banquet.

As it burns the body drops closer to the flaming wood, disintegrating in fire, ensuring its return to the elements.

Music sounds as the soul, represented by the red cord, is released.

Lempad's grandson has the honor of riding on the coffin to the six-tiered funeral tower.

All that remains of I Gusti Njoman Lempad are ashes and pieces of brittle bone, taken by his family to be dispersed in the sea.

THE DISSEMINATION OF RACHEL'S ASHES

They took Rachel's seven pounds of ashes out to sea on a boat from San Pedro, California. Three miles out, her husband and son carried out her last wishes: "Disseminate my remains at sea, without further ceremony."

Rachel had disliked the costly imposed rituals she had grown up with and never really celebrated the religious days anymore. Her husband and twenty-year-old son shared her disinterest in festivals and ceremonies. A few years before her death, Rachel had seen an advertisement for the Neptune Society, which promised simple funeral services at sea. She had filled out the form, added some personal instructions, signed an authorization for cremation, and informed her family of her wishes.

The boat stopped. Except for the seagulls, the lapping of the waves, and a light wind rippling the flag, it was peaceful and silent. Dr. Denning of the Neptune Society read a few appropriate words and his assistant scattered Rachel's ashes in the sea. Her husband tossed a small bouquet of flowers after them. The bottle of champagne stipulated in Rachel's instructions remained unopened.

THE BURIAL OF NEIL D. JONES

Neil D. Jones was a loner. When he died at home in his bed in Los Angeles, California, he left behind no close relatives or friends. Only a neighbor noticed that the quiet, seventy-four-year-old man, who kept mostly to himself, was not out gardening as usual and investigated.

It was discovered that Mr. Jones had left instructions for his interment at the Angeles Abbey Memorial Park. He wanted a dignified service and a serene place of burial. There should be, he stipulated, plenty of trees and, of course, lots of flowers. Mr. Jones left enough money for fresh buds to be placed on his gravesite at the turn of every season.

The service was as he requested, attended only by some neighbors and people Mr. Jones had worked with before he retired. The officiant delivered a eulogy to a quiet and honorable man. As the casket was lowered into the ground he reminded the gathering that all life on Earth dies—but always in proportion to that which is born.

SEASONAL CELEBRATIONS

You can feel them in the air, so closely are they related to the cycles of the Earth. Year after year they arrive, like welcome old friends, rekindling memories of childhood, generating excitement and interaction, decorating the world with their special symbols and moods. They are a revitalizing break in the routine of life—universal celebrations originally based on the cycles of the moon or the reaping of the harvest or the birth of a great nation or prophet. They keep the past alive, bringing together families, friends, and strangers with common heritages, reminding us of who we are and where we came from.

NEW YEAR'S EVE IN TIMES SQUARE

*T*here is nothing quiet or reverent about the crowd that gathers every New Year's Eve in Manhattan's Times Square, one of the city's seediest districts. Nearly a quarter of a million people converge—some drinking, some already drunk—to witness the official start of the year.

Seconds before midnight, way on top of a tall white building, a small electric ball descends a pole. The crowd chants a breathless countdown, then bursts into shouts of "Happy New Year!" as the ball completes its descent at the stroke of midnight and the number of the year flashes above a spectacular screen of computerized messages and images. Everyone is hugging and kissing wildly as strains of "Auld Lang Syne" fill the night. For better or for worse, another new year in New York has begun.

There is no crowd like the one that converges every year on Times Square to await the decisive hour of midnight. Nearly a quarter of a million people jam together in the bitter cold to welcome the New Year.

The crush of the mob can be both exhilarating and frightening. A lucky few find refuge atop a telephone booth at the corner of Seventh Avenue and 43rd Street.

Heralded by a parade of martial arts drill teams, costumed children lion dancers, and Miss Chinatown, the highlight of the celebration finally swirls down the avenue—the spectacular block-long dragon.

The dragon poses before the dignitaries in the reviewing stand. Its dramatically decorated head shakes wisely up and down before it suddenly starts spewing forth thunderous firecrackers that deafen everyone.

CHINESE NEW YEAR

ung hay fat chow!" is the Chinese greeting meaning "Happy New Year!" or, literally, "Wish you make a lot of money!" In San Francisco's Chinatown, as in other Chinese communities, it ushers in a month of festivities dominated by the balanced opposites of the world, yin and yang, farewell and renewal. The highlight of the celebration is the Parade of the Golden Dragon, held on the first night of the year. It follows a week of feverish preparations, including house cleaning, bill paying, and several symbolic yang-force gestures using noise and light to rout the evil spirits that have accumulated during the year.

The parade is a passing fantasy of shiny satin costumes, giant mythological puppets, prancing pompom girls, and marching bands. But nothing compares to the spectacular, block-long golden dragon—handmade of Chinese silk and velvet—kept in zigzag motion by thirty men and aglow by a generator in its tail section. A symbol of strength, it marks the end of one year and the beginning of another. Yin and yang, the balanced opposites, are forever active as the dormancy of winter is bid farewell to make room for the rebirth of spring.

NEW YEAR IN CHIENG-MAI

Wearing garlands of fresh orchids and scented flowers, the women of the city of Chieng-mai receive their New Year's drenching with laughter.

The New Year in Thailand comes in April, bringing a welcome warmth, for most people spend the three-day celebration drenched from head to toe! It is the Songkran or "water-throwing festival," marking the beginning of a new solar year in that part of Asia. All over Thailand, Cambodia, Burma, and Laos, water is flying everywhere! In the streets and in the homes, from tiny silver bowls and plastic buckets, the throwing of water symbolizes a washing away of the bad luck of the past.

The Thai New Year is also a time of cleansing—giving away or burning unwanted items—and of honoring ancestors, elders, and monks. Food is brought to the temples, statues of Buddha are bathed, and scented water is poured over the hands of parents and elders as a gesture of respect. On the second day there is a spectacular parade of dancers, beautiful girls, floats, and marching bands. As the festival comes to a close on the third afternoon, families gather—still soaking wet—to picnic on river banks alive with the sounds of splashing children and the aroma of freshly cooked food.

Knowing that the parade will end in the river, the smartest vendors claim their places early.

Small sand temples are built around statues of Buddha; birds are freed; incense and candles are burned.

BIANOU

In Africa, in the middle of the Niger part of the Sahara Desert, the small town of Agadés has been a gathering place since the ninth century. At the crossroads of the paths of the Fulani nomad tribe of cattle herders, the semi-nomadic Touareg traders, and the sedentary Haussa merchants, Agadés rises from the desert like a sand castle, a mirage that does not disappear.

The end of the winter season in Agadés, a time hotter than any Texas summer, is celebrated for three days during the first new moon of February. On the first day of Bianou, a local holiday, the town is awakened by the sound of distant drumming and the chanting of the *muezzin,* calling the faithful to prayer. As people gather in the dusty streets the drums begin to appear—first the large ones held by two men and pounded by another; then the smaller ones beat quickly by long-robed men. Behind them are the Touaregs, spinning around at incredible speeds. Their long blue robes are held in place by strips of embroidered leather; their turbans are wrapped and folded in a way that suggests a cock's comb—the cock symbolizing the awakening of the new season.

EPIPHANY

On the sixth of January, twelve days after Christmas, Christians commemorate the day the Magi—guided by the brightest star—found their way to the manger in Bethlehem where the infant Jesus slept. The Feast of Epiphany, which means "manifestation," recalls their visit, the day Christ was manifested to the world.

Also known as the Feast of Kings, Twelfth Day, and the Day of the Three Wise Men, Epiphany is the oldest festival on the Church calendar. In Mexico, as in Latin America and France, it is a joyous family day topped by a festive dinner. The high point of the meal is definitely the appearance of the traditional *galette des rois,* a delicious flat cake baked only on this occasion. Hidden in the cake is a broad bean or small porcelain infant figure that signifies good luck for the person who discovers it. Usually identified by a squeal of delight, the lucky one is crowned with a paper headpiece in a boisterous mock coronation. The new monarch then chooses a co-ruler by dropping the tiny ornament in someone's wineglass. Slightly embarrassed, the king and queen reign over an evening of laughter and warm camaraderie reminiscent of the two great festivals that still linger in the air—Christmas and the New Year.

CARNIVAL IN RIO DE JANEIRO

n all Roman Catholic countries, between Epiphany and Ash Wednesday, there is a period of revelry and feasting, a time of public holiday when work is forgotten and the streets are filled with people seeking pleasure and release . . . Carnival!

The people of Rio seem to begin anticipating the next Carnival the moment the last one ends. They prepare for it all year long, meeting periodically in their different carnival clubs, or "schools of samba," to plan their costumes and rehearse the steps they will perform in the glorious, competitive parade.

This year torrential rain poured down from darkened skies as the first school of samba assembled. Women in white-feathered bikinis and men in masks ran for cover as electrical systems crackled. But tropical rains during the Carnival season are short, and soon, to the delight of spectators, the sky began to clear. In the distance the sound of drumming could be heard.

Suddenly they appeared—thousands of men and women marching and swaying in languorous rhythm, painted and costumed in shimmering satin. Dancing and drumming, smiling and singing, reaching toward heaven, they were spurred on by the thunderous roar of the crowd. There were colorful floats depicting different themes, each one more outrageous and imaginative than the next. When the first school was finished, the judges deliberated before the second team began dancing down the avenue. And so it went, all through the night and into the next afternoon, until everyone was staggering from visual overload, physical exhaustion, and too much beer. Ecstatic and half-dressed, the revelers stumbled home —or to the beaches—to pass out for the rest of the day. But they would dance again that night to the samba sounds of street musicians. Carnival comes but once a year and there would be

plenty of time to rest later. Perhaps it is the anticipation of the stern season of Lent that infuses Carnival (*carne vale,* or farewell to meat) in Rio with a special kind of madness. All around the countryside, pranksters abound: men dressed as women, rustic clowns pounding each other with inflated pig bladders, disheveled undertakers, half-scary henchmen, crazed doctors in white masks and long surgical gowns, and nymphs in toga sheets. Children attend their own costume balls and dozens of mini Spidermen and Wonder Women can be seen whizzing about.

Ash Wednesday signals a return to business as usual and the beginning of the forty-six days of Lent, the period of Christian penance in preparation for Easter. But even in the most solemn of moments a smile of recollection may appear—along with a great idea for the next Carnival!

A group of veiled women honoring Iemanja, the goddess of the sea, dance by, wearing her colors and carrying objects associated with her. From dusk to early dawn Cariocans dance through the streets, raising the ambient temperature with their movements.

Unable to control their enthusiasm, the watching crowd jumps the barricades and invades the parade route, dancing wildly. Security clears the way for the next official group, a job they perform countless times during the night of festivities.

Gaily dressed clovis clowns have enlivened Carnival for centuries.

One clown waves an inflated pig bladder, ready to strike, bringing laughter from the crowd.

An undertaker poses with a miniature coffin filled with flowers and a retinue of toga-clad beauties.

Carnival is no time for inhibitions. Everyone indulges in their wildest fantasies as they dance down the long avenue in Rio de Janeiro on Parade Day.

The theme for this school of samba is Hannibal's triumphant crossing of the Alps.

A night of seasoned dancing gives way to the less sophisticated gyrations of the younger generation.

A gigantic snake of plumed Indians dressed in gold glides by at the close of this year's parade.

ST. VALENTINE'S DAY IN SAN FRANCISCO

The true origin of Valentine's Day, the festival of lovers, is uncertain. It has been celebrated as we know it since the fourteenth century, but may actually be a Christianized version of the Feast of Lupercalia, observed as far back as the third century in honor of the god Lupercus, who was supposed to protect Roman shepherds from wolves. There are at least eight historical figures with the name Valentine, seven of whom celebrate their feast day on February 14. One story says that the Valentine in question was a young Christian priest who secretly married young lovers during the reign of the cruel emperor Claudius who outlawed wedlock. Imprisoned, Valentine miraculously cured the jailer's daughter of blindness, which further enraged the emperor who had him beheaded on February 14. Another story says Valentine fell in love with the jailer's daughter and sent her love notes signed "from your Valentine." Whatever the true story, Saint Valentine has become the patron saint of lovers and February 14 a day to exchange messages of love in the form of flowers, gifts, cards, and candy wrapped in heart-shaped boxes.

In San Francisco, the heart, symbol of Valentine's Day, grows not only fonder on February 14, but sweeter and larger than life in the Embarcadero Shopping Center. Passers-by are invited to "have a piece of our heart" in the form of a hundred-square-foot carrot cake prepared by a local bakery. There is dancing to the music of Regency strings, and upstairs, in a division of the Museum of Fine Arts, there are workshops and demonstrations of how to make rubber stamps and silk-screened Valentine cards. Meanwhile, in the Hall of Flowers in Golden Gate Park, a senior citizens' Valentine's Day dance is in full swing.

ST. PATRICK'S DAY IN NEW YORK

Y ou don't have to be Irish to wear green on Saint Patrick's Day in New York City (even the Empire State Building's top thirty floors glow like an emerald) or to enjoy one of the city's most spirited parades. Since 1762, New Yorkers have been turning out on March 17 to watch their Irish neighbors march in honor of Saint Patrick, the patron saint of Ireland and of the Archdiocese of New York. They have cheered as the marchers follow the green-painted stripe up Fifth Avenue, past the majestic, century-old Saint Patrick's Cathedral, where a morning mass is held commemorating the young English lad who, in the fourth century, was kidnapped and brought to Ireland. Whether or not Saint Patrick actually chased all the snakes out of Ireland as some believe is uncertain, but it is known that he brought and spread Christianity there. Saint Patrick used the shamrock, the three-leaved clover that has since become a symbol of his day, to explain the existence of the Trinity.

From Saint Patrick's Cathedral the nearly 120,000 marchers, including school, police, fire, and military bands, citizens' and veterans' groups, and politicians, make their way through the nearly two million spectators to 86th Street. Usually there is a March nip in the air, which is the perfect excuse for a steaming hot cup of stiff Irish coffee. But for the most part no excuses are needed on Saint Paddy's Day, when whiskey flows like water and green beer is consumed by the barrel. It is the day, New Yorkers joke, that the Irish march up Fifth Avenue and stagger down Third!

HOLI IN JAIPUR

In the pink city of Jaipur, Rajastan, as everywhere else in northern India, the Holi celebration in March marks the end of the winter season. It is the most boisterous and colorful of India's thousand and one festivals.

"Namaste"—"I salute the divine in you." Extended families greet each other courteously in their private compounds, joining hands and bowing heads. Then swoosh! A plate of colored powder or a bucket of tinted water flies and, in a matter of minutes, the smiling faces change from green to shocking pink to brilliant red. It is the yearly ritual of Holi, symbolizing the advent of spring and all the colors dormant in nature now ready to shoot forth. It is a time of dressing up and dancing, of irreverence and uninhibited fun. For many, it also marks the beginning of a long period of cold baths, for in most homes water will not be heated again until winter returns.

On the evening before the color throwing, glorious bonfires commemorate the burning of the witch Holika, who once tormented all of India. According to legend, Holika, who was immune to fire, despised Prince Prahlad for his devotion to the god Vishnu and planned to destroy him by luring him into a blazing furnace. But the deities intervened and the magic was reversed. When the smoke cleared, Holika was just a pile of ashes on the furnace floor.

Large syringes filled with colored water are used to douse the guests.

A day of irreverence, on Holi not even the host and hostess can escape the ritual dousing with colored powder.

A quick bath in the fountain is a necessity after the symbolic dousing.

The beauty of spring is gaily welcomed with traditional music, herb drinks, stick dancing, and a rainbow of colors.

A gritty feeling follows the shock of being smeared with red powder.

Rose petals float in ochre-colored water vats; attendants frequently replenish the pink powder throughout the afternoon.

Dressing up in different costumes is part of the evening's festivities.

HOLY WEEK IN SEVILLE

*I*t begins with Palm Sunday, the day Jesus Christ rode triumphantly into Jerusalem while throngs of adoring followers carpeted his path with their cloaks and palm branches. It includes Holy Thursday, the day of the Last Supper, and Good Friday, the day of the Crucifixion. It culminates on the Sunday following the first full moon after the vernal equinox—Easter Sunday, the greatest day of the Christian year, the day of the Resurrection.

In Seville, Spain, the tradition of re-creating the events leading to Christ's death and resurrection dates back as far as the fifth century. Fifty-two religious brotherhoods carefully plan the week's activities that begin with a joyous Palm Sunday procession. Every day of the week the brotherhoods weave their way through the streets to the great Giralda Tower and Cathedral. Some carry *pasos,* or floats, on which magnificent statues—many by famous seventeenth-century sculptors—depict the Stations of the Cross. Others don the *penitente* habit to do their yearly penance by bearing candles before the *pasos.* Still others take their penance more literally. Barefoot, the *nazarenos* trudge behind the *pasos,* bent nearly in half under the weight of one or more large wooden crosses.

All of Seville leans from its windows and balconies to watch the processions and listen to the haunting music that accompanies them. Occasionally, a singer bursts into a passionate *saeta,* a song to the passing Christ or Madonna, who pauses under the window as if to listen. By far the grandest procession occurs on the night of Good Friday, when hardly anyone sleeps. At midnight, in total silence and darkness, a magnificent seventeenth-century sculpture —"Jesus del Grand Poder"—emerges from a small church to begin its journey to the cathedral. Dawn will see the Macarena, the favorite jeweled Madonna of the Sevillanos, come out of the Grand Portal, ending the Holy Week spectacular.

All of the members of the cathedral clergy are a part of the procession that takes place after mass on Palm Sunday morning.

Nazarenos walk behind the parade floats carrying wooden crosses as their penance.

To everyone's relief this pensive skeleton, the Canina *death figure*, leaves Seville on Saturday, the gloomiest day of the holy week.

Leaning from balconies and windows to watch the procession and listen to the music, all of Seville participates in the spectacle.

The exquisite Giralda Tower in Seville's main square is the center of Easter activity.

The seventeenth-century sculpture, Jesus del Grand Poder, *is carried from a small church to the cathedral at midnight.*

Elaborate floats depict the stations of the cross; statues of Christ and the Virgin are carried through the streets.

In a haunting scene hooded penitents walk for miles in front of the floats carrying candles as their yearly penance for their sins.

MAY POLE DAY

On the first day of May, with the chill of winter almost certainly gone, ancient spring fertility rites are reenacted by schoolchildren and neighborhood groups throughout England. They recall the days when, in grand processions from the woods, villagers brought sacred trees to the center of town. They raised them and feasted and danced around them in orgiastic celebrations of the renewal of spring.

In Castleton, England, on the eve of May Day, a chosen king is completely covered by a bell-shaped garland of flowers and led on horseback through the town. Reminiscent of the Green Man of European iconography, representing the growth of crops and all living things in the new season, this floral figure makes his way to the town church. There, the garland—except for a small piece known as the queen—is lifted from him and hoisted to the top of the steeple. Bands play as children dance around a maypole, weaving intricate designs with long, colorful ribbons. As the sun sets and the last notes of the bands die out, the "queen" is solemnly placed on the Castleton War Memorial.

Village school girls carrying posies and streamers assemble on the village square. The intertwining of dancers around the pole was originally symbolic of the integration of male and female energies.

On the eve of May Pole Day, a king for a day, hidden in a garland of wild flowers, is led through the streets of Castleton, England. A lady, also in Tudor costume, rides behind him until they reach the church.

MAY DAY IN PARIS

In continental Europe, May Day gradually evolved into a floral festival, a distant, lingering salute to the goddess Flora. In Paris and other urban areas the link to the past was a woman on a street corner with a basket full of fragrant lilies-of-the-valley. The sprig is given to family and friends as a symbol of good luck.

For many years, however, these delicate flowers have been eclipsed by the passing shadows of red flags and banners representative of Labor Day. For May 1 is Labor Day, or International Workers' Day, or Eight Hours Day, in sixty-six nations of the world. In Paris it has also become a time of protest—of all-day demonstrations of discontent and solidarity by workers and students. In Moscow it means a million people marching through Red Square in the largest military parade on earth.

Students, workers, political activists, and anyone who wants to gawk or march, take to the streets. Originally a floral celebration, May Day is also Labor Day and is celebrated with red flags as well as flowers.

Lily of the valley, the first of the spring flowers, has long been the traditional gift on May Day. These tiny bell-like flowers are sold by street vendors, like this woman in Paris, who seem to be fewer each year.

The celebration begins with the arrival of horse-drawn carts bringing sweet-smelling freshly mowed hay from the countryside.

Perched on delicate carriages, farmers await their turn at a game of skill—snatching rings from a post at a full trot.

The whole town dances to the tunes of the fiddler and the accordionist, just as their grandparents did before them.

The mayor, the hay queen, and their friends enjoy a traditional meal of rice and brandied raisins served in silver bowls.

HAY HARVEST

I t is the end of June. All the hay has been cut and stored away in the barns of Bolsward, Holland. The cattle's feed is assured for the winter. The milk the cows yield will be rich and full for hardy Dutch cheese. It is time for the yearly festival celebrating the abundant hay crop—the hay fest, beginning with a colorful parade fittingly led by a simple hay cart loaded with laughing children.

Later in the day farmers dress in their ancestors' finery and mount their restored nineteenth-century carriages for displays of driving dexterity and elegance past. The most skillful at the evening's driving competition returns home with a golden whip presented by local bank officials.

The second day of the hay fest features singing and folk dancing, culminating in the yearly hay meal shared by the entire community. The mayor, flanked by the hay queen and princess, is beaming. The speeches are a bit too long—perhaps anticipation of the country meal about to be shared by this gathering of harvesters and friends makes them seem so.

After being driven through the streets of Rothenburg in a horse-drawn carriage, the shepherd dancers gather at the main plaza.

The dancers heartily toast each other and drink to the memory of last year's harvest, as well as to the promise of this year's.

Hans could not bear to leave his pet duck behind, so the well-behaved bird joined wholeheartedly in the festivities.

As the clock chimes 2:00 P.M., the shepherd dancers take their first spirited steps in a folk dance in the town square.

WINE FEST

In the fields surrounding the town of Rothenburg, Germany, the sheep are grazing peacefully, but the shepherds have gone to town. Dressed in ancient finery, they are all-important on this day of the reenactment of the traditional Shepherds' Dance, celebrating the end of a historic epidemic.

July is also the time to clear the bottles of last year's wine in anticipation of the new wine harvest that is coming. This is one job that never lacks volunteers. Starting in the afternoon and continuing late into the night, there is drinking, toasting, and singing.

At the sharp call of the town crier's voice, the Shepherds' Dance begins. Men and women step in linear and circular formations, clapping and stomping gaily on the gray cobblestones of the town square. As the crowd looks on, centuries melt away before the colorful dancers and their traditional, rhythmic movements.

The older male members of the Santa Clara pueblo begin the ceremony with a long drum roll and a low-toned, but energetic chant.

The women hold their beat as the tribesmen weave in and out of their ranks, pounding the dirt in accelerating rhythms.

The women of childbearing age, dressed in traditional clothing, feathers, and jewelry, take their place in the center of the pueblo.

Clouds darken the sky and huge raindrops begin to fall on feather bonnets—the rain dance has fulfilled its ancient purpose.

Their cheeks dotted with red paint, the young maidens giggle behind their colorful eagle plumes as the men show off.

It's time to trade feathers for a nylon cap and jeans, as this young Indian goes off with his father, the tribal police officer.

GREEN CORN DANCE IN NEW MEXICO

In Santa Clara Pueblo, New Mexico, when the first green sprouts of corn push their way to the sun, the tribe gathers to invoke the protecting spirits and rain for abundant crops. Under the big tree in the center of the pueblo, the older men begin the Green Corn Dance with their great pounding drums. They are joined by the younger men, dressed and painted in their proudest colors, and the women of child-bearing age, holding feathers in one hand and brilliant desert paintbrush flowers in the other. The groups move from space to space, dancing and chanting as their ancestors have for centuries, heading for the sacred *kiva*. Then it becomes a game. Playfully, the braves block the maidens' way as they climb toward the sacred roof.

The Corn Dance is performed twice that day. As the dancers move toward the *kiva* for the second time, clouds darken the late afternoon sky and rain begins to fall. The dance has fulfilled its purpose; the corn will grow thick and sweet. The tribe has renewed its heritage.

SUMMER SOLSTICE
AT STONEHENGE

On the twenty-first of June, the shortest night of the year, the ancient order of Druids perform their summer solstice ritual at the prehistoric stone monument at Stonehenge, England. Sun worshipers may have gathered at the same spot nearly four thousand years ago.

For the thirty or forty men and women representing the Druidic order, the ritual begins with an hour's trek to an ancient mound south of Stonehenge for meditation. Meanwhile, on the grounds surrounding the monument, another kind of vigil takes place. Youthful spectators, with their rock music and mind-altering substances, come, as they have for twenty years, to camp out and experience the summer solstice.

It is nearly 3:00 A.M. when the Druids return, their faces framed by stiff hoods, their robes flowing and white. Silently they circle the outer limits of the monument, stopping at the four corners to leave behind people with symbols of the elements: air at the east; fire at the south; earth at the west; water at the north. Entering the stone structure, joining hands in a circle, they then begin to chant: "We are gathered here to bear witness to the power of the universal majesty, verity, and love infinite, according to the commands of the sacred fire." After a long, silent pose, a trumpet is sounded in four directions: north, south, west, and east. At exactly 4:40 A.M., as the last blast is heard, the sun in all its fiery glory rises above the northeastern stone, glowing warmly between the tall arches, illuminating the faces of the Druids.

Security is tight. A double row of barbed wire protects the monument from vandals. Only those with passes from the Department of Environment can get close to the structure. Camera crews are busy filming as the Druids silently file away, to return again at high noon for another ceremony.

THE FOURTH OF JULY

ireworks! That is what is most anticipated and remembered about the Fourth of July, a day with great historical significance. That was the day, in 1776, that representatives of the original Thirteen Colonies signed their Declaration of Independence from England. Today, in all the fifty states, as well as Puerto Rico, the Virgin Islands, and Guam, it is a day of summer's fun. There are picnics, like Willie Nelson's yearly gathering in Austin, Texas, parties, baseball games, and, with luck, a welcome long weekend. At night, in every town, displays of fireworks are organized and people enjoy spectacular sights and sounds.

In Philadelphia, where the Declaration of Independence was written and signed, reenactments of those historic moments take place each year. Although the famed Liberty Bell, located in the steeple of the Philadelphia State House, never really rang the announcement because it cracked in practice, bells sound across the nation: "Let freedom ring!"

BASTILLE DAY IN PARIS

reedom is also the theme of Bastille Day, the National Festival of France, celebrated on the fourteenth of July. That is the day in 1789 when the French masses stormed the infamous Bastille fortress, liberating political prisoners. Many a writer and revolutionary had been incarcerated there, simply on the word of a sealed royal mandate. When the Bastille fell, so did the aristocracy.

In Paris thousands of people turn out for a great parade on the Place de la Bastille or sometimes on the Champs Elysées, where the July Column, a tall bronze pillar holding a Mercury-like figure, now stands. It used to be a relaxed kind of spectacle, but now it has become a serious show of military discipline and equipment.

The fun really begins at night! For two consecutive days every district holds a free public ball, the most spirited being the Firemen's. Live bands play old Gallic tunes way into the night, stopping only for spectacular displays of fireworks. Children stay up late, chasing each other and tossing cherry bombs, while lovers of all ages dance in the streets that belong to the people until dawn.

WHEAT HARVEST

Planting and harvest festivals are among the oldest kinds of celebrations, dating back to ancient Roman times when they were performed to invoke the blessings of, and offer thanks to, various gods and goddesses. Chief among those venerated was Ceres, the earth mother, goddess of wheat. Her spirit is still honored today in the small village of Provins in the center of France, where, if the wheat harvest has been plentiful, villagers spend the last Saturday and Sunday of August rejoicing.

The villages are decorated with wheat and field flowers and there are exhibits of farming tools from centuries past. Braided straw dolls, like those played with by children in olden times, are made. In the late afternoon, after the heat of the day has passed, parades are held—processions of platforms on wheels and flatbed trucks appropriately pulled by tractors. Villagers reenact ancient rituals involving wheat and old methods of separating the grain, grinding it, and baking it into wholesome, delicious bread.

CHAMPAGNE HARVEST

Wine festivals in France can be traced back to the sixteenth century when the wine growers of Vevey formed a society that presented a spectacular parade on August 29, which occurred almost every year until 1889. Colorful and humorous floats carried elegant Swiss guardsmen, wine growers, shepherds, and representations of goddesses and gods, such as Diana, the goddess of the hunt and fertility, and Bacchus, the god of wine. Few people realize that Bacchus was also the god of vegetation and fertility. Afterward, there was joyous merrymaking, followed by festive dinners—served, of course, with great wine!

The spirit of the ancient wine festivals is echoed today in the most temperate regions of France where the champagne grapes grow, as in the village of Bar sur Aube. Smaller than ordinary wine grapes and picked earlier, their harvest is accompanied by a great celebration held before going into the fields, rather than afterward, when everyone is exhausted. Irreverence is the order of the day and every year a boisterous parade unfolds with fabulous floats, including one carrying an elegant young lady taking a champagne bath in an enormous tub made of flowers!

AFRICAN-AMERICAN DAY

African-American Day, organized in recent years by a local committee, celebrates a sense of community and cultural pride and achievement among the residents of Harlem. The main event of this early-September celebration is a parade, joined by local residents of all ages. Schoolchildren, senior citizens, marching bands, motorcycle clubs, police, politicians, civil rights and religious leaders, hospital and transit workers, businessmen, and entertainers make their way proudly down Adam Clayton Powell Avenue in a show of solidarity and community spirit. All heads turn to acknowledge the local government and community group leaders in the reviewing stand erected before the gleaming new post office at 125th Street.

COLUMBUS DAY

When Christopher Columbus first sighted fire on a darkened shore on October 12, 1492, he had no idea where his ship, the *Niña*, had landed. The shipmaster thought he had directed the sails toward India, so he dubbed the few astonished men who greeted them Indians. Neither he nor Columbus dreamed they were standing on the shores of a New World—on islands that would be called the West Indies, gateway to the Americas.

A national holiday honoring Columbus's discovery was established in the United States under the presidency of Franklin Delano Roosevelt in 1937. The day is also commemorated in most other North and South American countries, as well as in Portugal, Italy (the place of Columbus's birth), and Spain (the country that financed his expedition).

In New York City the annual Columbus Day Parade attracts thousands of patriots and parade lovers. Spectators line the sidewalks and sit on the curbs to watch schoolchildren, marching bands, police and firemen's units, and ethnic and professional groups move proudly up Fifth Avenue. Autumn is in the air. There are magnificent floats; the music is loud; the drums are exciting; the mayor is in the reviewing stand. Vendors are everywhere, hawking food, flags, balloons, buttons, and other souvenirs as Columbus sails through Manhattan.

SAN GENNARO FESTIVAL

![L]ittle Italy, lower Manhattan's Italian district, is always teeming with life, but for the past fifty-three years, for ten days beginning in the second week of September, it becomes a virtual anthill of activity. This colorful, fun-filled time draws thousands upon thousands of people to famous Mulberry Street to experience the sights, sounds, and mouth-watering tastes of the Festival of San Gennaro.

San Gennaro is the Italian name of Saint Januarius, the patron saint of Naples. September 19 is his feast day and it is joyously acknowledged worldwide, but especially in his home city and in Little Italy. Januarius is thought to have been martyred for his belief in Christianity during the persecutions that took place under Emperor Diocletian in the fourth century. A vial of his blood, collected after his beheading and preserved in the cathedral church of Naples, is said to turn from dust to liquid on his feast day and seventeen other times during the year. Many folktales and a popular cult have grown up around this miracle.

The San Gennaro Festival is, in the words of Mr. Tisi whose family founded it, a time "to pay homage to this miraculous saint." Dollar bills are pinned to his statues in acts of sacrifice and his relics are carried through the streets after a solemn high mass. There is a colorful parade and an annual lottery, but most people think of it simply as a joyous, noisy carnival of varied ethnic foods and music, games of chance, souvenirs, and curb-to-curb crowds!

HOMECOMING

f all the big weekends held at colleges and universities throughout the country, the biggest may be Homecoming, which takes place in the fall. This is the weekend the alumni return to visit their alma maters. Old friends and flames who have not seen each other for decades are reunited and revisit their old haunts, their old houses, the places where they learned, studied, and played. The weekend is usually the occasion of a big football game against the school's arch rival. All over campus, banners are hung, cheering the home team on. And of course there is the contest selecting the Homecoming Queen—the epitome of beauty and school spirit. She may be joined by a Homecoming King, usually an athletic hero. There are pep rallies, parties, concerts, bonfires, and, of course, the Big Game—hopefully followed that night by a victory dance!

The sound of flutes and horns fills the Fall air as the Homecoming Parade makes it way down Main Street in Seguin, Texas.

The seniors spend the day gathering fuel for a huge bonfire that everyone attends, along with parents and friends.

The cheerleaders hold a pep rally in the town's main square, firing up the fans and the players for the big game to follow.

The students and faculty dress in their finest for the homecoming dance, held in the specially decorated high school gym.

The homecoming team played their best game of the season, beating their archrivals in front of a cheering hometown crowd.

The homecoming king and queen are named at the dance, and the newly crowned couple enjoys the first dance of the evening together.

UNITED NATIONS DAY

F lags from every nation of the world fly together in front of the United Nations headquarters on the East Side of Manhattan. Despite the discord and deadlocks that go on inside, the very existence of such an organization—whose aim, according to the UN Charter, is the maintenance of international peace and security—is an accomplishment. In 1947 the General Assembly passed a resolution creating an official United Nations Day—October 24—commemorating the day the Charter was accepted by a majority of member nations in 1945.

United Nations Day is part of United Nations Week, seven days of ceremonies observed in some way in all the member nations. The purpose is to acquaint people with the aims and achievements of the international organization that, in addition to peacemaking, include the relief of hunger, disease, poverty, and illiteracy in underdeveloped nations. In schools, churches, libraries, and civic centers, activities are planned and concerts are held featuring songs and hymns from all over the world. This flag ceremony, honoring the United Nations, was performed by Boy and Girl Scouts in Indio, California.

VETERAN'S DAY
IN WASHINGTON, D.C.

From his wheelchair Max Cleland directs the affairs and fights for the rights of veterans in the United States. A former state senator in Georgia, Cleland won the silver and bronze stars for his service in the First Air Cavalry in Vietnam—but lost a great deal more. As Administrator of Veterans Affairs it is his privilege to place a wreath on the Tomb of the Unknown Soldier in Arlington National Cemetery on Veteran's Day. The ceremony—commemorating the ordinary G.I.'s who served in the two world wars, Korea, and Vietnam—takes place on the eleventh hour of the eleventh day of the eleventh month of the year—the time the Armistice of World War I was signed.

It was pouring rain when Cleland wheeled himself up to the tomb, placed the wreath, and paused in honor of America's thirty million living and fourteen million deceased veterans. A bugle played a noble taps as veterans and onlookers removed their hats, bowed their heads, and remembered. As the rain fell, a carillon rang for a full minute.

Afterward, everyone moved to an adjoining rotunda to listen to the United States Army Band music and to tributes and speeches about the special problems and future of veterans.

HALLOWEEN IN GREENWICH VILLAGE

Halloween—hallowed or holy evening—is the night when spirits rise and witches fly, when glowing pumpkins decorate doorsteps, and young and old dress up in costumes to party and trick-or-treat. A festival in black and orange—autumnal in spirit, eerie in mood—it enlivens the last day of October with customs and traditions drawn from a mixture of ancient beliefs.

In Manhattan's colorful Greenwich Village a new Halloween tradition is growing. For the past few years a costumed walk through the area has been loosely organized by Ralph Lee and a band of charming elves. Corpses, fairies, cackling witches, King Tut on roller skates, all dancing to the rhythm of lilting flutes, make their way down Fifth Avenue toward Washington Square. Suddenly, on top of the famous Washington Square Arch, bright red flares explode! Out of the smoke a grotesque ghost appears, dancing wildly, then plummeting to earth in a heart-stopping illusion. Hundreds of balloons and white doves rush toward the night sky in a final, spectacular display.

A pickup truck bearing a giant scarecrow is used to clear the streets, making way for the parade of goblins and ghosts.

This enthusiastic group offered Halloween treats from the back of their flatbed truck, which was equipped with a bar and piano.

A hay wagon filled with costumed children leaves Bank Street for an exciting ride through Greenwich Village to Washington Square.

This grotesque skeleton made its spooky appearance amidst a flood of bright red lights in Washington Square.

Costume creations range from the simplicity of grandmother's old dress to this elaborate handmade lobster costume.

Its original meaning lost to most twentieth-century celebrants, Halloween is now an occasion for parties, parades, and trick or treat.

THE JEWISH
FESTIVAL SEASON

Rabbi James R. Michaels recites the traditional Sukkot blessing for the lulav *and the* etrog *with his children.*

Many important Jewish festivals are celebrated during the months of September and October, which correspond on the Jewish calendar to the month of Tishri. The first two days are Rosh Hashanah, "the beginning of the year" and of the High Holy Days, a time of repentence, self-examination, and prayer. Jews believe that on Rosh Hashanah the Book of Life is opened and the fate of every individual is determined. That fate is sealed ten days later on Yom Kippur, "the Day of Atonement," the holiest day of the Jewish year.

In the middle of the month of Tishri comes Sukkot, a joyous seven-day festival commemorating the forty years of wandering in the desert endured by the Israelites after their release from bondage in Egypt. Modern Jewish families erect *sukkahs,* or booths, reminiscent of those used to shelter their ancestors.

The twenty-third day of the month is Simchat Torah, "rejoicing in the Law," when the yearly cycle of reading the Torah is completed and begins again.

Every year Rabbi Michaels builds a small booth outside his home in Queens, New York, to celebrate Sukkot.

The Whitestone Hebrew Centre is joyful during Simchat Torah, which celebrates the completion of the reading of the Torah.

THANKSGIVING

The Pilgrims of Plymouth, Massachusetts, who started the American tradition of giving thanks after the autumn harvest, had good reason to be grateful. They had survived a grueling forty-day voyage aboard the *Mayflower* and a bitter winter in a strange new land that claimed the lives of nearly half their members. By the end of the summer of 1621 they even had corn and other crops to harvest. Governor William Bradford set aside the thirteenth of December as a day of feasting and prayer.

One day stretched into three. Beneath the late autumn sky, at long wooden tables laden with food, the settlers gathered with eighty Indian friends. There were contests of strength and skill, races, and military displays led by Captain Miles Standish. There were songs, sermons, and prayers of thanks—for the corn and other sweet vegetables; the meat, fish, and fowl; the berries from which they made sweet wine; and for just being alive.

Thanksgiving became a regular holiday in 1863 thanks to Sarah Josepha Hale (author of "Mary Had a Little Lamb") whose impassioned editorials prompted President Lincoln to set aside the last Thursday in November as a "day of thanksgiving." This practice held until 1939, when President Roosevelt moved the day ahead a week to give businessmen the benefit of a longer Christmas shopping season. In 1941 Congress silenced the ensuing protests by legally establishing the fourth Thursday in November as Thanksgiving Day.

Today, Thanksgiving is a family holiday, a day for coming home. Wherever home is, the menu is the same—candied sweet potatoes, fresh green peas, creamed onions, cranberry and apple sauce, cider, pumpkin pie, and, of course, that magnificent turkey!

At the Pound Ridge Reservation members of the staff reenact the first Thanksgiving.

At home in Vermont the Millman clan says grace before enjoying the plentiful autumn bounty. Thanksgiving has retained its original meaning and remained relatively unchanged by commercialism.

MACY'S THANKSGIVING DAY PARADE

It is the eve of Thanksgiving. All night long, in the streets surrounding the Museum of Natural History in New York, workers from Macy's department store are busy preparing the most imaginative parade of the year. Enormous animals, unequaled even by the famous dinosaurs inside the museum, are being blown into life with helium for one glorious day. In the morning they will transform Central Park West into a larger-than-life fantasy come true.

The Macy's Thanksgiving Day Parade has been a tradition since 1924. It starts at 9:00 A.M. at 75th Street with the spectacular appearance of Mickey Mouse, Bullwinkle, Snoopy, and other favorite characters, four stories high! Joined by colorful and elaborate floats, it moves to 34th Street, past Macy's block-long, block-wide store. It celebrates both the spirit of Thanksgiving and the official beginning of the Christmas season. Santa makes his first appearance of the year in a luxurious red-and-white sleigh, ending the parade.

Kermit the Frog, asleep the rest of the year, is blown up much larger than life for the spectacular Macy's Thanksgiving Day Parade.

With the museum as a backdrop, this group, carrying large papier-mache puppets, prepares to take its place in the parade.

The first in line after the starting band, Leo the Lion peeks around 76th Street before leading the helium animals downtown.

Surrounded by pumpkins and Pilgrims, actor Mickey Rooney waves jubilantly from the back of an enormous Thanksgiving turkey.

Everybody's favorite moose, Bullwinkle, has a panoramic view as he glides four stories above the streets of New York City.

On the last float in the parade, Father Christmas ushers in his own season, pulled by his twelve famous reindeer—and a truck!

HANUKKAH

hen Alexander the Great conquered the Persian Empire in 336 B.C., he placed Palestine under the rule of a succession of Syrian kings. In 175 B.C., Antiochus Epiphanes—nicknamed "the madman" by his closest advisors—came to power and began one of the darkest periods in Jewish history. "I am God," he would roar, and all were expected to bow down and worship. When the Jews refused he destroyed their Temple, defiled their altars, and had them brutally murdered.

In the hills of Palestine, despair and desperation flared into rebellion. A Jew named Mattathias killed a Syrian soldier who had sacrificed a pig on a Jewish altar. He then fled to the mountains with his five sons to form a guerrilla army. Untrained, ill equipped, hopelessly outnumbered, these Maccabees, as they came to be known, toppled the Syrian forces, then reentered Jerusalem.

They found their Temple in ruins—scrolls torn, altars red with the blood of animals, and idols everywhere. They cleaned and purified and, on the twenty-fifth day of the lunar month of Kislev, rededicated the Temple to Jewish worship and relit the Eternal Light using the only holy oil they could find—enough to burn for one day.

Miraculously, it burned for eight. Jews celebrate that miracle every year with the festival of Hanukkah, which means dedication. Every night for eight nights as a blessing is recited, another candle is lit, and the menorah that holds them is placed in a window. Families gather for festive meals of *latkes* (potato pancakes) and special puddings. Hanukkah *gelt* (money) is won and lost in lively spins of the *dreidel,* a four-sided top. And, of course, there are presents—one for each night—to the great delight of the children!

HANUKKAH
IN
NEW YORK

The seven-branched menorah was a symbol of Judaism long before the miracle of Hanukkah happened. It decorated the holy tabernacle in the desert and lit the great Temple of Solomon. At its center is the Star of David, a visible link with Judaism, embellished in ancient times by the pomegranate fruit, a symbol of rain and the many "seeds," or children, of Israel. The Hanukkah menorah was especially designed to commemorate the time a tiny jar of oil miraculously burned for eight days. It has seven branches plus a special place for the *shammash,* or servant candle, from which all the other wicks are lit.

For the past few years the world's largest menorah, thirty feet high by twenty-four feet wide, has been erected at the crossroads of Manhattan—Fifth Avenue and 59th Street. Strikingly modern, the three-story structure is built by a Lubavitch youth organization. On the first night of Hanukkah a cherry picker lifts the officiating rabbi to the top to kindle the first light with a one-foot candle. After the blessing the rabbi addresses the crowd, describing the ceremony as a chance "for the people of this great city to enjoy the flavor and spirit of the festival of lights." Afterward there is traditional music, dancing, and singing that lasts into the night.

AID AL-MAWLID

The anniversary of the birth of the Prophet Muhammad is celebrated as a great event throughout the Muslim world. Local customs and differences between Muslim sects determine the festivities in each location, but one event is common to them all—the recitation of the Koran, the sacred text containing the revelations made to Muhammad by Allah Himself.

In the Moroccan capital of Rabat, where the king resides for part of the year, a four hundred-year-old ritual is faithfully observed during the Aid al-Mawlid. Turkish in origin, the dramatic "wax procession" was brought to Africa by the corsairs (pirates), and it falls to the descendants of their prisoners to carry on the tradition. The *barcassiers,* as they are called, arrive in the morning from the ancient city of Salé. Dressed in hand-embroidered costumes reminiscent of their ancestors, they go to the house of the waxmaker to view the immense wax totems they must carry through the streets of the city.

Faithful to the Muslim tradition of showing no lifelike representations, the motifs that make up the sculptures are geometric patterns. A religious leader arrives to bless the participants as they struggle to lift the totems. Wavering beneath their enormous weight, they wind their way through the narrow streets of the old city's *casbah,* accompanied by drums and flutes.

As they near the center of town the streets get wider and the crowd grows more excited. The royal guard stands at attention as a younger son of the king arrives to preside over the festivities. The *barcassiers* are joined by splendid horsemen, artisans, farmers, and even a bride on a horse, in a parade that ends with an evening of cleansing and prayer.

Twelve days after the first new moon of spring, the multicolored wax sculptures are paraded through the streets of Rabat.

In front of the old stone ramparts, the Royal Guard salutes as the king's son arrives to preside over the day's festivities.

On the Prophet Muhammad's birthday, prayers are recited outside the wax artisan's home.

Tents are set up throughout Morocco for fantasias as riders show off their mounts, such as this finely harnessed Arabian horse.

The thunder of hooves and rifles is mixed with the shrill cries of the riders as they display their skill with guns and horses.

CHRISTMAS IN OAXACA

It is the most joyous of Christian holidays, eagerly awaited and colorfully celebrated in 105 nations. Christmas, the anniversary of the birth of Jesus Christ, commemorates the time Joseph and Mary came all the way to Bethlehem from Galilee to register for a census. With all the inns full, they were forced to take shelter in the manger where Christ was born. The simplicity of the setting in which this extraordinary person came to the attention of the world has lived on through twenty centuries of transforming cultures. Every year crèches are set up in churches, with straw on the floor and figures of Joseph and Mary. At the midnight mass held on Christmas Eve, a tiny infant figure is carried through the darkened churches, followed by a candlelit procession. Worshipers burst into song as Jesus is placed with his family.

Not everything about Christmas is so simple. It can be a hectic, maddening, crowded time of shopping and commercial pressure. One might become cynical were it not for the faces of the children as they catch their first glimpse of Santa, dream of what they'll get, hang their stockings, gaze at a beautifully decorated tree, or open their presents on Christmas morning.

Christmas in Mexico is a public fiesta. Dozens of Santas set up shop in the streets to be photographed with children. There are recreations of the holy family's search for lodging, fireworks, brightly wrapped presents, and *piñatas,* papier-mâché figures that, when broken, shower sweets and gifts on the children. In Oaxaca, sixty kilometers south of Mexico City, there is the famous festival of the radish artisans. Indians carve incredibly intricate figures and construct beautiful scenes of the Nativity and passions of Christ from the flesh of this simple vegetable.

The week before Christmas, the owners of radish stands in the Oaxaca market do a brisk business selling to local artisans.

On Christmas Eve, floats carrying cherubic youngsters and lit with colored lanterns add to the festive spirit.

On the night of December twenty-third booths are set up along Zocalo Plaza, where the radish sculptors display their Nativity scenes.

The rest of the family follow the brightly lit Nativity parade through the streets of Oaxaca with their newborn children.

Bunuelos, *sweet fried pancakes, are a favorite holiday treat. The bowl in which they are eaten is broken to avoid bad luck.*

The three-day feast ends with fireworks and a midnight mass in the cathedral. Seraphic little figures attend—if they can keep their eyes open.

ELEMENTS, OBJECTS, AND DEVICES

A flag waving in the breeze, a joyous feast, flowers, candles, costumes, music, parades, presents, prayers—these are some of the universal elements, objects, and devices, the symbols of celebration. They are the ornaments, the atmosphere, part of the birth-to-death rituals that dress up a day and make each one different. They excite the senses, evoke associations, and establish connections between the past and present; mediate between the individual, nature, society, and God. They are the difference between eating simply to satisfy hunger and feasting—the fine china, the silver, the toasting, the guests. They add richness and dimension to celebrations and a new vitality to life.

The most basic elements of celebrations are the most basic elements of life—Air, Fire, Earth, and Water. Ether, known as the fifth element, represents space and the eternal nature of all living entities. It is considered the invisible link between vibration and form. These elements have always been a symbolic part of festivals and ceremonies because they are intrinsically involved in the most basic human ritual of all—survival.

AIR

Air, the elusive element, surrounds and sustains life. It is the most immediate and vital of the basic elements—without breath, there is no life; without wind, seeds are not disseminated; without Air, there is no Fire. Symbolic of liberty and fluid movement, it helps create and carry a mood—an atmosphere—evoking feelings and physical sensations that will forever be associated with the event that is occurring. In its active form, Air is wind, gentle and cleansing, but it is also capable of violence.

In certain ceremonies, Air is symbolically placed to the east, corresponding to spring, infancy, dawn, and the crescent moon.

FIRE

From the earliest days of humanity, the sun has been worshiped as the preeminent sustainer of life, its seasons determining all action. Fire, manifested by flames, light, and heat, is symbolic of the sun's emanation on Earth. It represents energy essential to life and transformation. Through it, material passes from one form to another—symbolically, from this world to the beyond. In its constructive form, Fire, like the sun, produces heat and light to ward off cold, darkness, and death. Torches, candles, bonfires, Fire festivals, even Christmas lights all were originally linked to rituals assuring the continued activity of the sun against darkness. In its destructive form, Fire rages, terrifies, consumes, and annihilates, whether as a blazing inferno or a single stunning bolt of lightning. Punishment by Fire has long precedent in the history of humankind. But Fire also symbolizes regeneration —the phoenix rising out of the ashes, for example.

Fire is symbolically placed to the south, representing summer, youth, the heart, midday, and the full moon.

EARTH

s the ultimate source of all food and shelter, the Earth has always been associated with fertility and growth—personified as the great sustaining mother, Mother Earth. Fertility and agricultural rites are among the oldest types of human rituals, performed at planting, when the first young shoots appear, and again at harvest. These rites are directed toward the maintenance and increase of the food supply upon which the community is dependent. In its darker moods, the Earth claims back the lives it has nourished, through earthquakes and volcanic eruptions. The sustaining mother, who provides food for her people, can become a devouring entity, a taker of lives, with a need for bodies in her soil to feed herself.

Earth is symbolically placed to the north, corresponding to winter, old age, night, and the new moon.

WATER

hether cascading over silvery cliffs, pouring from the sky as cooling rain, or flowing in patterns analogous to the course of human existence, Water is symbolic of purification, fecundity, regeneration. A body immersed in Water as in a ritual baptism undergoes a symbolic dissolving and death, returning with renewed vitality and cleansed of sin. Pilgrimages often center around Water sources, and ceremonies of all faiths and cultures are held beside them to draw upon their soothing ions. The Hindus hold bathing in the Ganges river at dawn as most sacred; Christian services begin with the sprinkling of holy Water; Muslim prayers are never uttered before the prescribed ablutions; and, at the time of death, the *taharah*, or ritual washing of the body from head to toe, is central to the Jewish faith. In its constructive form, Water cools, cleanses, replenishes, and renews. When aroused or excessive, as in floods or tidal waves, it can wipe out entire civilizations. It is associated with disorder and is a bad omen when it is agitated, like a furious sea, or poisonous, as in stagnant Waters.

Water is symbolically placed to the west, corresponding to autumn, middle age, evening, and the waning moon.

LOCATION

Many celebrations were originally held around a natural site that served as both a gathering place and a reminder of the wonders of god.

The couple that chooses to be married in an elegant Manhattan ballroom has a different vision than the one that exchanges vows on a sun-covered hillside. The location of a ritual or celebration says a lot about the nature of the participants and the spirit in which the act is undertaken. Places also create their own spiritual and sensory associations, contributing strength and inspiration to a ceremony.

Beneath the open sky, beside a towering tree or a majestic mountain, vows gain new significance, festivities seem all the more vibrant. There is a feeling of simplicity, of order and perfection that the ancients likened to the sacred landscape of God.

To contain and confront God more intimately, people have always constructed sacred places, from simple tents to elaborate houses of worship. Entering a church or temple is like turning inward spiritually, to contemplate and emerge reawakened. There is a sanctity, a reverence to vows undertaken in a blessed location, just as there is an intimacy and warmth to rituals performed at home.

Artificial structures, whether an exotic temple or a simple tent, define celebratory spaces and set them apart.

The location of holy places is carefully chosen, for it must reflect the nature of the shrine it hosts.

BANNERS

They thrust forward authoritatively, into the air, into the wind, heralding the day's activities. They fly at the top of tall poles and masts, at the head of parades, on cars and rooftops, representing a group, a country, a group of countries, a club, a custom, a cause. Bright, colorful collages of cloth, exalting the spirit and essence of those who fly them. Or, perhaps, they carry words or symbolic art, like so many prayers fluttering in the wind, summoning the spirits and divine forces.

During the Sonkran festival in Thailand, dazzling, narrow banners brighten the streets and are rallying points for the crowd.

Leading a parade, this Dutch woman has a chance to publicly show her own patriotic sentiments as she carries her country's colors.

The prayer flags that decorate the Bodhanat stuppa in Nepal are there to send their messages to heaven on the ascending winds.

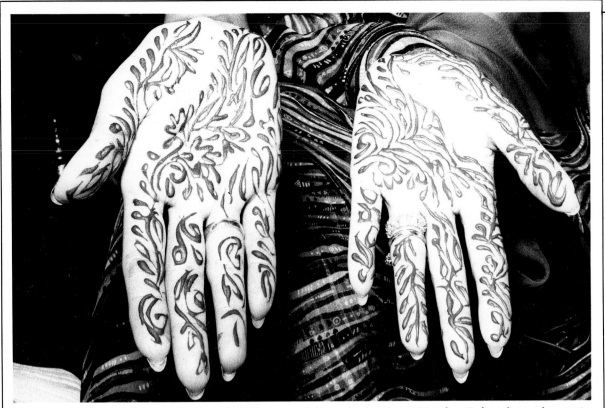

In the mendi *ceremony, an integral part of the Hindu wedding, the bride-to-be and her female friends spend an entire day being adorned with intricate henna designs, applied by artists who make such designs their life's work.*

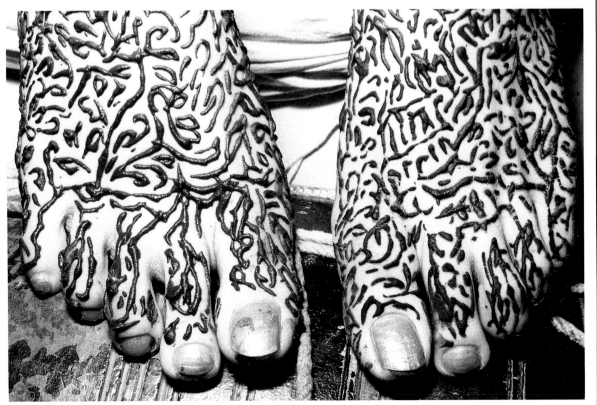

Body designs can serve as invocations and as talismans to ward off any harm that might befall their wearers. Designs mark individuals going through rites of passage and also designate a member of a group.

ADORNMENT

Celebration and decoration go hand in hand. On the great occasions of our lives we decorate our homes, our churches, our windows, our streets, and, most intimately, ourselves. We adorn our bodies with elegant, traditional, or fanciful clothes that make us feel special and that reflect the mood and spirit of the day. And in all cultures we undergo the elaborate ritual of applying makeup.

The intricate designs that are drawn on the palms and feet of the Hindu bride and all her female guests on the morning of the wedding announce to the world that they have participated in a great event. The dye of the cooling henna plant lasts for one month before fading away. Brilliant body and face designs, tattoos, and scarification are also popular as symbols of strength and transformation—in American Indian rituals, in Africa at initiation time, and in the tribal war games of New Guinea. In the case of the Western woman trying to enhance her beauty for the special moments of her life, the games are more subtle, and so is the makeup. In death, one last touch of rouge may be applied before the funeral begins.

Clothes and other adornments affect and enhance celebrations. Their color and texture add to the spirit and significance of the occasion. Elaborate headpieces, precious minerals and stones, flowing robes and formal gowns, not only set the tone of a gathering but greatly influence the mood and behavior of the participants. In part it is the actual feel and visual impact of the cloth and ornaments—denim is a far cry from silk. In part it may derive from the ancient idea that adornments are but external symbols of inner spiritual feelings.

Colors also serve as symbols; each evokes its own associations—white of purity, red of passion, black of mourning and death. In religion, alchemy, heraldry, literature, and art, certain colors are connected with specific seasons, holidays, moods, or events. In general, the warm, advancing tones—yellow, orange, red, white, and gold—are associated with moments of assimilation, activity, and intensity. The cold, retreating colors—blue, silver, violet, and black—are linked to times of distance, debilitation, and passivity.

Shrouded in gold and mother-of-pearl costumes that capture and cast off the sunlight—precious metals and stones are always associated with deities—these Balinese dancers parade in celebration of their warriors' valor.

Wearing the prescribed robes of the United Methodist Church, and flanked by a similarly clad deacon, the Reverend Brown conducts a communion service for his devout Watts, California, congregation.

MASKS

laring, golden, fearful, frozen symbols of transformation, masks can be the catalysts for combining human and divine spirits, or they can be invested with their own mystical powers, like statues and talismans associated with deities. When used in dance they can personify those powers, as well as different moods and forces. They can also personify demonic tendencies, as with carnival masks, which are frequently inspired by images of the netherworld. Through them, the wearer publicly reveals and releases his own baser tendencies, a practice that may derive from rites of exorcism in which masks become liberating mediums, allowing tortured fantasies to run their course.

The Western tradition of wearing masks on Halloween can be traced back to ancient Druidic practices. The Druidic *Samhain* or New Year, which fell on November 1, was the time the dead were believed to return to mingle with the living. After feasting with the ghosts, villagers donned masks representing the souls of the dead and paraded to the outskirts of town, luring the spirits away.

The supernatural golden façade of this worshipper at an interfaith mass in New York jolted a few of the participants.

This Halloween mask reveals four faces of humanity, letting the reveler temporarily transcend his human limitations and feel, like the god Janus, that he can serve both as an anchor for humanity and a seer of his, and our, fate.

LIGHTS

*I*llumination plays a major part in setting the mood of a celebration. Light in its purest form, Fire, is symbolic of spiritual presence. In a single flame dancing at the end of a wick, one senses God's relation to the individual, like the flame to the candle, separate but inseparable.

Candles are lit for meditation and prayer, at baptisms, and on birthdays. When they are blown out it is not to symbolize a rejection of the past, but rather a burst of hope for the future, to manifest the persistance of the breath of life. They glow at vigils, church services, funerals, and in processions, indicating a spiritual presence and conveying people's prayers and offerings through the ethereal vibration of the flame.

Torches suggest guidance—through the fires of Hell, through initiation rites—and continuity, as in the torch that ignites the Eternal Flame at the Olympic Games. Bonfires derive from Japanese festivals of lanterns, or *Bon,* when they were lit to welcome the dead, who were believed to visit Earth at that time. There are also festivals of light in India, after the monsoons, when tiny oil lamps are set afloat upon the rivers; and among Jewish people who kindle the Hanukkah menorah. The Easter candle in the Catholic Church represents the departure of Jesus' soul, while the glow of multicolored Christmas lights seems to rekindle the summer sunlight in the midst of winter darkness.

By day, by night, flames flicker—fragile like human hope, burning like human love.

FOOD

F ood is a symbol of abundance, the natural culmination of a season or celebration. Many rituals were originally performed to assure the continued abundance of food or to give thanks for the harvest. The symbol of a fruitful harvest is the cornucopia, the horn of abundance, spilling over with natural gifts of grains, vegetables, and fruits. The horn was believed to have been broken from the head of Amalthaea, the she-goat who nursed the god Jupiter when he was a child. Jupiter made one of her horns into the cornucopia, promising that it would always be filled with the foods she loved. He also set her image among the stars as the constellation Capricorn. Birthday cakes, the most universal of celebratory treats, are a gathering of harvest foods—grain, fruit, and milk—creating a delicious and traditional dish that is reminiscent of the moon cakes offered to deities in earlier times.

Planning, preparing, serving, and savoring food are a major part of celebrating. Religious rules, such as Jewish kosher laws and Hindu vegetarian precepts, sometimes play a part, ensuring purity and the proper relationship between people and God. Ritualistic offerings of food and drink before beginning a feast or holy day service are common in Japan and other Eastern nations, echoed in the West by saying grace. One ritual offers tangible examples of the best of what humanity has sown, the other offers thanks for the fruits of our labor.

"There is no joy without wine!" declares the rabbi as the couple he is marrying shares a glass during their traditional Hebrew ceremony. The Japanese agree—the drinking of saki is part of their Shinto marriage sacrament. Toasts are drunk at nearly every celebration. Wine, during the Mass, is also a powerful Christian symbol, representing the blood of Christ. Hydromel, or liquid honey, is another ritual drink, served during the annual pagan feast of Samain for its pure and strengthening qualities. When the elders of the Bambaras Tribe in Africa drink fermented hydromel, their words are believed to come from a wiser, more mellow place.

Birthday cakes are always accompanied by the traditional slicing ceremony in which the honored person slices his piece first, and in so doing symbolically separates himself from his past, and from the others.

In Japan no ceremony is complete without the placing of food on an altar to show respect for the gods.

DANCE

Dance is liberating. Dance is spontaneous. Dance is the language of the subconscious. On an individual level dance is the manifestation of inner life and thoughts, the expression of beauty and self-knowlege through graceful, rhythmic, sensuous movements. On a spiritual level it is the abandonment of the body to divine manipulation. Group dances symbolize unity through the linking of hands or arms in a chain. When a circle is formed, as in a round dance, energy is circulated among the dances, offering protection and generating feelings of strength and warmth.

Dance can be an appeal to the gods, like the Hopi rain dance; it can be a test of endurance, like the Apache sun dance; it can lighten the load of the possessed, like the medicinal Voodoo trance; it can be a joyous social affair or a ritual of deliverance, like certain carnival dances through which the darker side of the soul is symbolically revealed and destroyed.

Spontaneous or ecstatic dance also has a place in ceremonies, but it cannot be choreographed or controlled. While it brings an element of disruption to orderly ritual, it can also give it new life, allowing a personal, creative, and exuberant expression to surface.

VEGETATION

Vegetation is symbolic of solar energy transformed by the earth into magnificent expressions of joy, devotion, nourishment, life, and death. Vegetation is the living symbol of celebration; used as a decorative element, it often becomes part of the ritual or ceremony as well.

Trees link the three levels of the cosmos: the depths of the earth into which the roots are burrowed; the surface of the earth, from which the trunk and branches spring; and the sky and the heavens, which are brushed by the highest leaves and branches. Laurel, cypress, oak, palm, and, of course, evergreen, are symbols of perpetual life.

Plants, which possess the ability to renew themselves, are also symbols of growth and regeneration.

Flowers are the sensuous gifts of the earth, representing harmony and love. Their purity and brevity are reminiscent of childhood, and the beauty and pleasure they give evoke the Garden of Eden. Flowers are also the images of spiritual growth, blossoms of inner development, and their colors parallel the great variety of human emotions.

Medicinal herbs and plants are used in rituals for their curative and poisonous powers. They are used to induce altered states of consciousness, heighten sexual awareness, release inhibitions, and spark intellectual creativity. Cults have been formed around the potent peyote plant of Central America and the ayahuasca vine of the Amazon basin.

A plant can grace any room, bringing warmth and animation to the dimmest nooks and crannies.

These simple objects—plants, flowers, and an egg—make up a religious offering in Nepal.

The placing of flowers on graves is both an act of devotion and an acknowledgment that life, like a bloom, is far too short.

SCENTS

Related to the general symbolism of the air by which they are carried, scents and aromas evoke both spiritual and sensory awareness. Their ethereal quality is reminiscent of spiritual presence and the nature of the soul. The ascending fumes of incense, used in many Eastern and Indian rituals, are considered to elevate prayers to heaven or, in yoga practice, to open doors of perception and measure the time of meditation. The burning of incense can also be viewed as a sacrifice or as a purifying agent that cleanses the atmosphere.

Less symbolic, but just as evocative, are the aromas of cooking food, drifting from the kitchen to the waiting gathering of celebrants, or the fragrance of freshly cut flowers on the table, the acrid smell of tobacco, sensuous perfume, and other familiar human scents. They linger in the air evoking warm and pleasant memories long after the celebration is over.

Frankincense resin, which the Three Wise Men brought to the manger, is placed into the handcrafted thurible, or incensor, where it will burn slowly. The use of incense is common to most religions, where it serves both a practical and symbolic purpose.

The leader of the service carries the thurible, swaying it gently to disperse the scent. The slowly swirling ascent of smoke symbolizes the rising of prayers to heaven, and its scent cleanses and purifies, setting the holy place apart from all others.

AMULETS

mulets, talismans, and charms, also known as gris-gris, are among the most popular methods of ensuring good luck around the world. They are part of many ceremonies in which protection is sought, in general or from specific dangers such as illness, drought, crop failures, wounds, battles, accidents, and evil spirits.

Amulets derive their supernatural powers from their different symbolic and magical associations. Generally small, they are considered to work best when kept concealed and revealed only at critical times. Talismans are believed to develop a rapport between their owners and the forces they represent. Charms are magic formulas that are sometimes sung or recited in the direction of the talisman in order to ensure the desired result.

Many of the decorative objects adorning altars, statues, or human bodies today derive their inspiration from the ancient Egyptian practice of covering mummies with gold, bronze, and porcelain amulets in order to ensure immortality. The scarab, an insect once revered for its ability to decompose matter and help create new life forms, is still popular today. The divine eye, suggesting the ever-knowing presence of God, set in a triangle suggesting the Trinity, such as the one represented on the dollar bill, is a talisman against the evil eye. The number five, associated with the human figure, also appears often in talismanic invocations: the five daily prayers, the five keys to secret knowledge, the solemn oath repeated five times. Some other universal symbols of luck and protection are naturally perforated stones, arrowheads, teeth, claws, horns, shells, human hair and bones, beads, coins, crosses, bells, medals, and scribal art. The power of the amulet lies not so much in the object itself as in the force projected onto it.

These cherubic figures, mediators between humanity and outside forces, carry the responsibility of freeing their wearers from life's pitfalls and tragedies, while bringing them good luck and happiness.

Religious articles often serve as amulets, warding off the evils in this world, as well as keeping their wearers safe for the next.

PRESENTS

They are piled under Christmas trees, they highlight birthdays, and are bestowed upon brides and grooms, hosts and hostesses, sweethearts and spouses, newborn babies, retirees, mothers, fathers, graduates, and more! Presents—carefully chosen, beautifully wrapped, modern-day offerings expressing love, congratulations, and thanks.

Presents take many forms, but perhaps the most universal is money. Although some feel it is cold and impersonal, the giving of money actually has a rich spiritual tradition. Feast days activate a flow of currency that contributes to the distribution of wealth. The Japanese visiting a Shinto shrine know that money is one of the media between them and the divine. As they toss a coin or drop a bill into the collection box in the temple, they concentrate and clap their hands to attract the attention of the deities. The Chinese believe one way of ensuring good fortune is to slip a few bills into lucky red-and-gold envelopes and distribute them to family members. In the Christian Church the offering of eucharistic bread and wine is accompanied by the giving of alms. Alms giving is also one of the five precepts of the Muslim faith. Money can be lucky. Coins have always had talismanic associations, especially gold ones that reflect celestial light.

Celebrations and human rites of passage are a time to give—to each other, to God, to charity. In addition to being an expression of love and thoughtfulness, presents and gifts of money are symbols of sacrifice, of letting go of one's precious possessions.

The townsfolk convene before their mayor's mansion in Thailand to celebrate the solar New Year. They give presents of thanks, small remembrances, and tokens of their best wishes for another good year.

The Feast of San Gennaro is celebrated not only by impassioned eating but by the giving of gifts.

STATUES AND IMAGES

 tatues and images have always been at the center of celebrations, giving shape and form—although at times abstract and ideal—to deities, spirits, and beliefs. Icons are not really considered divine in themselves, but pathways to the divine, more like windows between earth and heaven, open both ways.

Statues are not considered effective until they are placed—usually in churches, shrines, public plazas, or on domestic altars—and consecrated with the proper invocation. Their symbolism lies not only in their forms but in the materials from which they are made. Stone conveys strength and unity, as in the great megaliths at Stonehenge or the black meteorite, the Kaaba, kissed by every Muslim pilgrim to the Great Mosque at Mecca. Gold is likened to celestial light; other metals, in addition to being precious, are chosen for their curative powers.

Drawn and painted religious images are not considered created, but transcribed by human hands from the divine, according to an ideal nature. The Virgin Mary iconography was originally attributed to Saint Luke. The image of Buddha was said to be the result of lifting his shadow from the ground.

Religious images, whether in humble human or more fantastic forms, allow worshippers to focus their thoughts and prayers.

Statues of gods, goblins, saints, or madmen bring their subjects forcefully to life.

Abstract images can both please the eyes and tease the brain with their swirling designs, their vitality, and their illusionary movement.

RELICS

*I*n Western culture the thought of keeping relics—remains of past family members in the form of ashes or parts of the body—seems eerie and primitive. Such age-old customs and rites connected with commemorating the dead are rapidly disappearing in societies where death and the disposal of bodies is an agonizing process. Yet ancestral worship is a long and honored tradition.

Skeletons, skulls, ashes, and fragments associated with saints and martyrs have particular significance. The personification of death and, sometimes, demoniacal forces, skeletons also represent the short spell of life on earth, the knowledge of one who has traveled the unknown and pierced the secrets of the beyond. Although in our culture, with its lighthearted association to Halloween, skeletons have more humorous than serious connotations, in other cultures they are revered. Hindus view skeletons as the permanent survivors of living beings, receptacles of their spirit and thoughts. Their tradition of cracking the skull to ensure the soul's final release stems from this belief. In other cultures they imply asceticism and immortality.

The skull, vault of the brain, center of all spiritual and physical activity, is likened to the sky of the human body. It is a symbol of strength. In Tibet and Nepal skulls are fashioned into artifacts essential to tantric rites: dagger, bone flute, sacrificial knife, skull drum, skull bowl, and bone apron.

Ashes of the dead are kept in urns, symbolic of the womb, the first and last abode of a person on earth. The Sadhus of India cover their naked bodies with ashes in a gesture of humility. Christians echo the thought on Ash Wednesday, when the foreheads of Catholics are signed with the ashes of palm leaves to remind them of their origins: "Remember, you are dust, and to dust you will return" (Genesis 3:19).

PRAYER AIDS

*T*here are prayers of devotion, meditation, repentance, adoration, gratitude, and supplication. Prayer aids are used to guide the worshiper, key the memory, increase concentration, and intensify the rituals of worship and meditation.

One of the most powerful and universal aids to prayer is the written word. Passages from sacred texts, when repeated aloud or in silence, alone or in chorus, provide inspiration and revelation and also seal human ceremonies. Prayers are sometimes murmured with each bead of a rosary, with prayer wheels, on prayer rugs, or beside symbolic paintings and drawings. Rosaries are thought to create a link between the supplicant and the divine; prayer wheels reflect the power of the scriptures; prayer rugs represent sacred spaces; sand and earth drawings are a form of symbolic language representing the deities and their attributes.

Prayer aids take other forms, for example, the ram's horn or *shofar* used to call Jewish people to prayer. Some think its purpose is to disorient Satan. Others say its plaintive, primal blast is a way of sharpening a worshiper's sensitivity or awakening those who have grown complacent in their devotion to God.

One hundred and eight wooden prayer beads and a small book of supplications accompany this pilgrim on his quest.

The blowing of the shofar, *or ram's horn, on Rosh Hashanah ushers in the Jewish New Year with confidence and ceremony.*

Sand diagrams, drawn for invocation and prayer, are found not only in Haiti but in a multitude of cultures throughout the world.

VESSELS

Like the urns that hold the ashes of the dead, vessels, removed from the context of their practical purposes, are strongly suggestive of the womb. In the presacrificial offering of the Ifugaos of the Philippines, there is definite sexual symbolism—the jar corresponds to the passive, the spear to the active. Yet that is only one of the many symbolic associations evoked by vessels, containers, and utensils.

The chalice, which received the blood of Jesus Christ, appears throughout mythology, from the medieval quest for the Holy Grail to the ritual libations during the Eucharist. Cups and glasses are also symbolic of the maternal breast and its flow of nourishing liquid. Pots, pans, pitchers, vessels for purification and ablutions, vats and vials of holy oil, terracotta jars containing sulfur, salt, and other symbols of strength—all represent abundance, the outpouring of elements unleashed by the rituals.

There is an ambivalence to the symbols of utensils in the form of weapons that frequently appear in ceremonies. On one hand, they are symbols of strength and the determination of the human spirit. On the other, they are purveyors of destruction. The sword, for example, appears in benign form, as in the ritual cutting of a birthday or wedding cake, establishing a positive cut with the past, and in violent form, as when used by the Japanese *Samurai* to slay the monster within in the ritualistic act of hara-kiri. When balanced on the heads of belly dancers, it is a reminder of the courage displayed by tribeswomen who fought off savage attackers while their men were fighting elsewhere.

ALTARS AND SHRINES

![dropcap S] hrines and altars are among the sacred spaces that have always been constructed by people to reach, meet, or house the divine. Shrines are special places or receptacles for sacred relics and representations—structures consecrated to and sometimes considered the abodes of spirits or deities. They can be massive, ornate buildings like the famed Angkor Wat of Cambodia, or simple homemade arrangements of photographs, flowers, and candles. Some shrines are portable, carried by parishioners on festive or ceremonial occasions to places where they are thought to bring blessings and good luck. The Japanese believe that deities, represented by mirrors, are enshrined in the elaborate *mikoshis,* or tabernacles, which processioners make dance and rise like the phoenixes affixed to their tops.

Altars are raised structures or mounds upon which religious rites are performed and toward which worship and meditation are directed. Altars symbolize the places on earth where human beings can enter the realm of the divine. On them, or nearby, sacrifices are made in symbolic pleas—petitions to God—but also as gifts honoring God, and as gestures of thanks.

Far removed from their original sites, these altars sit incongruously on a beach in Rio de Janeiro for New Year's Eve rituals.

Monsieur Vincent, a priest, and his wife sit in the humphor, *or mystical center of their compound, surrounded by ceremonial objects.*

While carrying the mikoshi, *or shrine, through the streets of Tokyo, the porters move to the beat of the drums.*

PLATFORMS

A moving platform not only thrusts the figures it carries closer to heaven but it takes those figures away from plodding, human movements and into the realm of mystical, effortless travel, letting them glide above the crowd.

By elevating a shrine, raising a throne or the chairs of honored people, or lifting and carrying religious and symbolic characters and scenes, platforms identify the central figures and symbols of an occasion. Platforms are used to honor these symbols and figures, at least for a while, by raising them above mere mortals and bringing them closer to heaven.

Although the motor hearse has replaced the ancient funeral chariot and the flatbed truck has taken over for once straining muscles, platforms still move through crowds on days of celebrations as they have for centuries. Carrying the symbols of the day, they create dramatic and colorful impressions. Every viewer has his or her own special moment as these sacred and spectacular sights pass before them, exalted on platforms. Their movement through the crowd suggests the passage of time, the human parade or procession through the seasons and through life.

Platforms are used to venerate people and religious and symbolic characters, or scenes, by raising them closer to heaven. Viewers have their own special visions as the sacred or spectacular sights pass before them on platforms.

MUSIC

usic extends human communication to the divine, or spiritual, realm. It brings forth emotions not often tapped in the daily routine and touches parts of the human spirit that words cannot reach.

Every instrument has its own symbolism and produces its own particular response. The powerful metallic blast of a trumpet heralds the beginning of great events in a burst of expectation and strength. Bells, symbolic of mystic and protective powers, toll for moments of joy, sorrow, danger, and death. Certain bells are invested with powers of exorcism, capable of chasing away evil spirits, while others help elevate souls to heaven. Flutes have a hypnotic, mellowing effect—soothing, spiritual, and haunting, yet also playful and merry. The *ney,* or reed flute, accompanies the trance of the whirling dervishes in their Dhikr dance, where the soul expresses its longing for reunion with the divine source. Tibetan cymbals, African bull-roarer, Brazilian maracas, Jewish fiddle, Irish lyre, Hindu conch, guitar, accordion, piano, drum, and many other instruments all contribute their sounds to the emotions that cannot be expressed with words.

Symbolic of the first breath of life, singing is an expression of the inner self. Like music, it is an exaltation of feeling, intensified by the bonding of individuals in joyous or solemn spiritual chorus.

The sound of the drum, that quivering, primordial sound, almost like the sound of a quickened pulse, can enter into listeners' hearts, forcing them to beat faster, breaking down their civilized resistance, capturing them within its rhythm.

Carpio and his peers from the Taos pueblo have grown up with the beat of drums, as have their parents and their parents' parents. The drum beat, slow and cautious or fast and urging, has always been part of the ceremonies of their tribe.

PERPETUAL CALENDAR

JANUARY

Movable Days

Meitlisunntig
(*Switzerland*)
Magh Mela Fair
(*Hindu*)
Ta-uchi (*Japan*)

Black Nazarene Fiesta
(*Philippines*)
Chinese New Year*
(*USA*)

*or February

1	2	3	4	5	6	7
New Year's Day Independence Day (*Haiti*) Anniversary of the Emancipation Proclamation (*USA*)	Day of the Revolution (*Cuba*) Hero's Day (*Haiti*) St. Berchtold's Day (*Switzerland*)	Feast Day of St. Genevieve (*Roman Catholic*) Lucretia Mott's Birthday	Louis Braille's Birthday Sir Isaac Newton's Birthday Independence Day (*Burma*)	Epiphany Eve or Twelfth Night (*Christian*) Anniversary of installation of first woman governor (*USA*)	Feast of the Epiphany, or Three Kings' Day (*Christian*) Army Day (*Iraq*)	Christmas (*USSR*) Ganna, or Christmas Day (*Ethiopia*) Pioneer's Day (*Liberia*)
8			9	10	11	12
World Literacy Day Feast of St. Gudula (*Belgium*)			Feast Day of St. Julian (*Roman Catholic*)	League of Nations founded in 1920 First session of the United Nations General Assembly in 1946	Independence Day (*Chad*) Eugenio Hostos's Birthday Proclamation of the Republic Day (*Albania*)	John Hancock's Birthday
13			14	15	16	17
Tyvendedagen—Twelfth Day after Christmas (*Norway*) St. Knute's Day (*Sweden*)			Albert Schweitzer's Birthday New Year's Day (*Russian Orthodox*)	Martin Luther King's Birthday Seijin-no-hi or Adult's Day (*Japan*)	Samuel McIntire's Birthday	Feast of St. Anthony (*Roman Catholic*)
18	19	20	21	22	23	24
St. Peter's Chair Day (*Roman Catholic*) Santa Prisca Day (*Mexico*) National Revolution Day (*Tunisia*)	Theophany (*Russian Orthodox*) Edgar Allan Poe's Birthday Lee–Jackson Day (*USA*)	Feast Day of St. Sebastian (*Roman Catholic*) Army Day (*Mali*) Grandmother's Day (*Bulgaria*)	Feast Day of St. Agnes (*Roman Catholic*) Anniversary of the death of Lenin (*USSR*)	Ukrainian Day (*USSR*) Feast Day of St. Vincent of Saragossa (*Europe*) Francis Bacon's Birthday	The Birthday of the Grand Duchess (*Luxembourg*)	Alacitis Fair (*Bolivia*) Anniversary of the discovery of gold in California (*USA*)
25	26	27	28	29	30	31
Robert Burns's Night (*Scotland, England, Newfoundland*) Feast of the Conversion of St. Paul (*Christian*)	Australia Day Duarte Day (*Dominican Republic*) Republic Day (*India*)	Feast Day of St. John Chrysostom (*Christian*) Mozart's Birthday	Jose Marti's Birthday Democracy Day (*Rwanda*)	Thomas Paine's Birthday Anton Chekhov's Birthday	Holiday of the Three Hierarchs (*Russian Orthodox*) Franklin Delano Roosevelt's Birthday Mohammed's Birthday (*Islamic*)	Independence Day (*Nauru*) Franz Peter Schubert's Birthday

FEBRUARY

Movable Days

Thaipusam *(Hindu)*
Tibetan New Year
Baika-sai *(Japan)*
Shrove Tuesday*
(Christian)

Ash Wednesday*
(Christian)
Pre-Lenten carnivals*
(Christian)

*or March

1
Langston Hughes's Birthday
Feast Day of St. Brigid *(Roman Catholic)*

2
Candlemas Day *(Roman Catholic and Christian)*
Ground-hog Day *(USA, Canada)*
James Joyce's Birthday

3
Fiesta of San Blas *(Puerto Rico)*
Elizabeth Blackwell's Birthday
Bean-throwing Festival or Setsubun *(Japan)*

4
Independence Day *(Sri Lanka)*
Anniversary of first Winter Olympic Games

5
Constitution Day *(Mexico)*
Feast of St. Agatha *(Malta)*

6
New Zealand Day

7
Charles Dickens's Birthday
Independence Day *(Grenada)*

8
Narnk Sun Pageant Day *(Norway)*
Jules Verne's Birthday

9
Amy Lowell's Birthday
Feast Day of St. Apollonia *(Roman Catholic)*

10
Mother's Day *(Norway)*
Boris Pasternak's Birthday

11
Thomas Alva Edison's Birthday
Youth Day *(Cameroon)*
Armed Forces Day *(Liberia)*
Foundation Day *(Japan)*

12
Abraham Lincoln's Birthday
Charles Darwin's Birthday
Union Day *(Burma)*
Independence Day *(Chile)*

13
Fiesta de Menendez *(Florida, USA)*

14
Valentine's Day *(Great Britain, France, USA, Canada)*
Viticulturists' Day *(Bulgaria)*
Copernicus' Birthday

15
Galileo's Birthday
Susan B. Anthony Day *(USA)*

16
Independence Day *(Lithuania)*

17
Anniversary of the organization of the National Congress of Parents and Teachers in Washington, D.C. *(USA)*

18
Independence Day *(Gambia)*
Constitution Day *(Nepal)*

19
Constitution Day *(Gabon)*
Martyrs' Day *(Ethiopia)*

20
Anniversary of the death of Klas Pontus Arnoldson *(Sweden)*

21
National Mourning Day *(Bangladesh)*
Anniversary of the death of Malcolm Little *(USA)*

22
George Washington's Birthday
Mother's Day *(India)*
Unity Day *(Egypt and Syria)*

23
Republic Day *(Guyana)*
George Frederick Handel's Birthday

24
Feast of St. Matthias *(Christian)*
National Day *(Estonia)*

25
National Day *(Kuwait)*

26
Victor Hugo's Birthday

27
Independence Day *(Dominican Republic)*
Independence Day *(St. Kitts and Antigua)*

28
Burgsonndeg *(Luxembourg)*
Kalevala Day *(Finland)*

29
Leap Year Day
Gioacchino Rossini's Birthday

MARCH

1	2	3	4	5	6	7
Feast Day of St. David Independence Day *(Dominica and St. Lucia)* Constitution Day *(Panama)*	Independence Day *(Morocco)* Alexander Graham Bell's Birthday	Liberation Day *(Bulgaria)* Martyrs' Day *(Malawi)* Hina Matsuri, or Doll's Festival *(Japan)*	Feast Day of St. Casimir *(Poland and Lithuania)* Constitution Day *(USA)*	Independence Day *(Equitorial Guinea)*	Independence Day *(Ghana)*	Feast of St. Thomas Aquinas *(Roman Catholic)* Tomas Masaryk's Birthday

8	9	10	11	12	13	14
Women's Day *(USSR and China)* Independence Day *(Syria)*	Feast Day of St. Catherine *(Bologna)* Taras Shevchenko Day *(Ukraine)*	Anniversary Salvation Army *(USA)*	Johnny Appleseed Day *(USA)*	Independence Day *(Mauritius)* Moshoeshoe's Day *(Lesotho)* Girl Scout Day *(USA)* Birthday of King of Libya	Joseph Priestley's Birthday Decoration Day *(Liberia)*	Albert Einstein's Birthday

15	16	17	18	19	20	21
Ides of March Thanksgiving Day *(Honduras)*	James Madison's Birthday	St. Patrick's Day *(Ireland)*	Sheelah's Day *(Ireland)*	St. Joseph's Day *(Roman Catholic)*	Lajos Kossuth Day *(Hungary)* Independence Day *(Tunisia)*	Bach's Birthday Benito Pablo Juarez's Birthday Vernal Equinox

22			23	24	25	26
Arab League Day *(Egypt, Iraq, Saudi Arabia, Lebanon, Syria, Yemen)* Emancipation Day *(Puerto Rico)*			Republic Day *(Pakistan)*	Agriculture Day *(USA)*	Feast Day of the Annunciation *(Roman Catholic, Anglican, Lutheran)* Independence Day *(Greece)*	Independence Day *(Bangladesh)* Prince Kuhio Day *(Hawaii, USA)*

27			28	29	30	31
Resistance Day *(Burma)*			Teacher's Day *(Czechoslovakia)*	Independence Day *(Maldive Islands)* Boganda Day *(Central African Republic)* Martyrs' Day and Youth Day *(Taiwan)* Vietnam Veteran's Day	Vincent van Gogh's Birthday Francisco de Goya's Birthday Seward's Day *(Alaska, USA)*	Rene Descartes' Birthday Haydn's Birthday

APRIL

Movable Days

Palm Sunday*
  (*Christian*)
Passover* (*Jewish*)
Easter Sunday*
  (*Christian*)
Buddha's Birthday

Feast of A-Ma (*China*)
Maha Thingan Festival
  (*Burma*)
Nagasaki Takoage or
  Kite Flying Contest
  (*Japan*)

*or March

1
April Fool's Day *(USA)*
Sergei Rachmaninoff's
  Birthday

2
Hans Christian
  Andersen's Birthday
International Children's
  Book Day
Emile Zola's Birthday

3
Anniversary of the
  beginning of the
  Pony Express *(USA)*
Washington Irving's
  Birthday

4
Feast Day of St. Benedict
  (*Roman Catholic*)
Liberation Day
  (*Hungary*)
Senegalese National Day
  (*Senegal*)
Anniversary of NATO

5
Tomb-Sweeping Day
  (*Taiwan*)

6
Chakri Day (*Thailand*)

7
World Health Day
Yugoslav Republic Day
  (*Yugoslavia*)

8
Anniversary of death of
  El Greco (*Spain*)

9
Martyrs' Day (*Tunisia*)
Baudelaire's Birthday

10
Humane Day (*USA*)
Joseph Pulitzer's
  Birthday

11
Battle of Rivas Day
  (*Costa Rica*)
Fast and Prayer Day
  (*Liberia*)
Resistance Movement
  Day (*Czechoslovakia*)

12
Space Probe Day (*USSR*)

13
Songkran Day
  (*Thailand*)
Independence Day
  (*Chad*)

14
Feast Day of St. Justin
  (*Roman Catholic*)
Pan American Day (*Haiti
  and Honduras*)

15
Leonardo da Vinci's
  Birthday

16
Feast Day of St.
  Bernadette
  (*Roman Catholic*)
Queen Margrethe's
  Birthday
De Diego Day
  (*Puerto Rico*)

17
Independence Day
  (*Syria*)
Children's Protection
  Day (*Japan*)
Independence Day
  (*Cambodia*)

18
Anniversary of Paul
  Revere's Ride (*USA*)

19
Feast Day of Blessed
  James Duckett
  (*Roman Catholic*)
Independence Day and
  Day of the Indian
  (*Venezuela*)

20
Daniel Chester French's
  Birthday

21
Brasilia Day (*Brazil*)
Kartini Day (*Indonesia*)
Natale di Roma (*Italy*)

22
Immanuel Kant's
  Birthday
Nikolai Lenin's Birthday
Earth Day

23
Feast Day of St. George
  (*Christian*)
William Shakespeare's
  Birthday
National Sovereignty Day
  and Children's Day
  (*Turkey*)

24
Armenian Martyrs' Day
  (*Turkey*)
Secretaries' Day (*USA*)

25
Feast Day of St. Mark
  (*Mexico*)
Liberation Day (*Italy*)
National Flag Day
  (*Swaziland*)

26
Union Day (*Tanzania*)

27
Independence Day
  (*Togo*)
Independence Day
  (*Sierra Leone*)
Second Republic Day
  (*Austria*)

28
James Monroe's Birthday

29
Emperor's Birthday
  (*Japan*)

30
May Day Eve,
  or Maitag Vorabend
  (*Switzerland*)
Walpurgis Night
  (*Finland and
  Scandinavian
  countries*)

MAY

1
International Workers'
Day
Lei Day *(Hawaii)*
May Day *(Turkey,
Great Britain, USA)*

2
Peasants' Day
(Burma)
Feast Day of St.
Athanasius
(Roman Catholic)
Education Day
(Indonesia)

3
Constitution Day
(Japan)
Constitution Day
(Poland)
Feast of Our Lady of
Czestochowa
(Poland)

4
Mother's Day
(South Africa)
Horace Mann's
Birthday

5
Liberation Day
(Ethiopia)
Karl Marx's Birthday
Tango-no-sekku,
Children's Day
(Japan)

6
Sigmund Freud's
Birthday
Martyrs' Day
(Lebanon)
Shepherds' and
Herdsmens' Day
(Bulgaria)

7
Johannes Brahms's
Birthday
Spring Day *(Scotland)*

8
World Red Cross Day
Feast Day of St.
Michael *(Roman
Catholic and
Anglican)*

9
Victory Day *(USSR)*

10
Commemoration of
National Institutions
Day *(Cameroon)*

11
International Mother's
Day

12
Constitution Day
(Cambodia)
Florence Nightingale's
Birthday
Garland Day
(Great Britain)

13
Jamestown Day *(USA)*
Sir Arthur Sullivan's
Birthday

14
Kamuzu Day *(Malawi)*
Unification and Inte-
gration Day
(Liberia)
Constitution Day
(Philippines)

15
Feast Day of St. Isidore
(Mexico and Spain)
Feast Day of St. Dympna
(Belgium)

16
William Henry
Seward's Birthday
Swami Muktananda
Paramahansa's
Birthday

17
Independence Day
(Norway)

18
Feast Day of St. Eric
(Sweden)
Flag Day *(Haiti)*

19
Ho Chi Minh's
Birthday
Flag Day *(Finland)*
Youth Day *(Turkey)*

20
Independence Day
(Cuba)
Independence Day
(Saudi Arabia)
Mecklenburg Day
(USA)

21
Navy Day *(Chile)*
The Anastenarides
Feast *(Greece)*

22
Republic Day
(Sri Lanka)
Sir Arthur Conan
Doyle's Birthday

23
Labour Day *(Jamaica)*
Anniversary of the
German Federal
Republic

24
La Fete de Saintes
Maries *(France)*
Day of Slavonic Letters
(Bulgaria)

25
Freedom Day *(Chad,
Zambia, Mauritania)*
Independence Day
(Jordan)
Day of Youth
(Yugoslavia)

26
Independence Day
(Guyana)

27
Independence Day
(Afghanistan)
Children's Day
(Nigeria)
Freedom and Consti-
tution Day *(Turkey)*

28
Memorial Day
(Puerto Rico)
Feast of St. Augustine
*(Roman Catholic
and Anglican)*

29
John F. Kennedy's
Birthday

30
Feast Day of St. Joan
of Arc *(Roman
Catholic)*
Memorial Day *(USA)*
Countee Cullen's
Birthday

31
Union or Republic Day
*(Union of South
Africa)*

JUNE

Movable Days

Pentecost (*Christian*)
Queen Elizabeth's Birthday
Father's Day
Tano Festival (*Korea*)

Dragon Boat Festival (*Chinese*)
Intiraymi-Sun Festival (*Peru*)

1	2	3	4		5
Children's Festival Day (*Republic of China*) Madaraka Day (*Kenya*) Constitution Day (*Tunisia*)	National Day (*Italy*) Youth Day (*Tunisia*)	Memorial to Broken Dolls Day (*Japan*)	Flag Day of Armed Forces (*Finland*) Commonwealth Day (*Botswana*)		Feast Day of St. Boniface (*Roman Catholic*) Constitution Day (*Denmark*) World Environment Day (*UN nations*)
6	**7**	**8**	**9**		**10**
Constitution and Flag Day (*Sweden*) Memorial Day (*South Korea*) Annual Sibelius Festival (*Finland*)	Foundation Day (*Western Australia*)	Anniversary of the death of Mohammed	Feast Day of St. Columbia (*Ireland*)		Camoes Memorial Day (*Portugal*)
11	**12**	**13**	**14**	**15**	**16**
The King's Birthday (*Nepal*) Kamehameha Day (*Hawaii, USA*) Ben Jonson's Birthday	Helsinki Day (*Finland*) Independence Day (*Philippines*) Peace of Chaco Day (*Paraguay*)	William Butler Yeats's Birthday Feast of St. Anthony of Padua (*Portugal*)	Flag Day (*USA*) Mother's Day (*Afghanistan*)	Magna Carta Day (*Great Britain*) Valdemar's Day (*Denmark*)	Feast Day of the Madonna (*Italy*)

17
National Day (*Iceland*) James Weldon Johnson's Birthday

18		**19**	**20**	**21**	**22**	**23**
Evacuation Day (*Egypt*) Waterloo Day (*Great Britain*)		Blaise Pascal's Birthday Independence Day (*Kuwait*) Artigas Day (*Uruguay*)	Independence Day (*Senegal*) Flag Day (*Argentina*)	Feast Day of St. Aloysius (*Roman Catholic*) Summer Solstice	President's Day (*Haiti*) Schoolteacher's Day (*El Salvador*) Feast Day of St. Alban (*Great Britain*)	National Day (*Luxembourg*) Midsummer Eve or St. John's Eve (*Finland*)
24	**25**	**26**	**27**	**28**	**29**	**30**
Bannockburn Day (*Scotland*) Day of the Indian or Dia de Indio (*Peru*) Nativity of St. John the Baptist (*Roman Catholic*)	San Juan Day (*Puerto Rico*)	Independence Day (*Malagasy Republic*) Independence Day (*Somalia*)	Helen Keller's Birthday	Mnarja Folk Festival Day (*Malta*) Jean Jacques Rousseau's Birthday	The Feast of St. Peter and St. Paul (*Roman Catholic*)	Revolution Day (*Guatemala*) Independence Day (*Zaire*)

JULY

Movable Days

Reed Dance Day
(*Swaziland*)

Feast of Lanterns or
Bon Festival
(*Japan*)

Tenjin Matsuri
(*Japan*)

1

Dominion Day
(*Canada*)
Republic Day (*Ghana*)
Heroes' Day (*Zambia*)
Half-Year Day
(*Hong Kong*)

2

Visitation of the
Blessed Virgin Mary
(*Roman Catholic*)

3

Independence Day
(*Algeria*)

4

Independence Day
(*USA*)
Garibaldi Day (*Italy*)

5

Peace and Unity Day
(*Rwanda*)
Independence Day
(*Venezuela*)

6

Republic Day (*Malawi*)
Anniversary of the
death of Jan Hus
(*Czechoslovakia*)

7

Feast Day of St. Cyril and
St. Methodius
(*Christian*)
Saba Saba Day
(*Tanzania*)

8

Anniversary of the First
Passport (*USA*)

9

Independence Day
(*Argentina*)

10

John Calvin's Birthday
Army Day (*Albania*)
Independence Day
(*Bahama Islands*)

11

National Day (*Mongolia*)
Bawming the Thorn Day
(*Great Britain*)

12

Orangeman's Day
(*Northern Ireland*)

13

Night Watch or La
Retraite (*France*)

14

Bastille Day (*France*)
African Community Day
(*Senegal*)
Republic Day (*Iraq*)

15

Feast Day of St. Vladimir
of Kiev (*Christian*)

16

La Paz Day (*Bolivia*)
Feast Day of our Lady of
Mt. Carmel (*Christian*)

17

Constitution Day
(*South Korea*)
July Revolution Day
(*Iraq*)
Melvin C. Hazen
Avocado Festival
(*USA*)

18

Labor Day (*Spain*)
Day of National
Mourning (*Mexico*)
Constitution Day
(*Uruguay*)

19

Independence Day
(*Laos*)
Martyrs' Day (*Burma*)

20

Independence Recogni-
tion Day (*Tunisia*)

21

Schoelcher Day
(*Martinique*)
Martyrs' Day (*Bolivia*)
Independence Day
(*Belgium*)

22

National Liberation Day
(*Poland*)

23

Revolution Day (*Egypt*)
National Day (*Oman*)

24

Bolivar Day (*Ecuador
and Venezuela*)
Valencia Fair (*Spain*)

25

Independence Day
(*The Netherlands*)
Guanacaste Day
(*Costa Rica*)

26

Revolution Day (*Cuba*)
Independence Day
(*Liberia*)
Independence Day
(*Maldive Islands*)

27

Barbosa Day
(*Puerto Rico*)

28

Independence Day
(*Peru*)
Somers Day (*Bermuda*)

29

Feast Day of St. Olaf
(*Norway*)

30

Marseillaise Day
(*France*)

31

Feast Day of St. Ignatius
(*Roman Catholic*)

AUGUST

Movable Days

Esala Perahera
(Sri Lanka)

Independence Day
(Jamaica)
Awa Odori, The Fools'
Dance *(Japan)*
Pajjusana *(Jainist)*

1	2	3	4	5	6	7
Army Day *(People's Republic of China)* Independence Day *(Benin)* Fiesta Day *(Nicaragua)* Herman Melville's Birthday	Feast of the Virgin of the Angels *(Costa Rica)*	Independence Day *(Niger)*	Peer Gynt Festival *(Norway)*	Independence Day *(Upper Volta)*	Independence Day *(Bolivia)*	Discovery Day *(Trinidad and Tobago)* Battle of Boyaca Day *(Colombia)*
8	**9**	**10**	**11**	**12**	**13**	**14**
Woman's Holiday *(Nepal)*	National Day *(Singapore)* Sanus; Army Day *(Libya)*	Independence Day *(Ecuador)*	Independence Day *(Chad)* Coronation Day *(Jordan)*	Youth Day *(Zambia)*	Women's Day *(Tunisia)* Queen's Birthday *(Thailand)*	Independence Day *(Pakistan)* Victory Day *(USA)*
15	**16**			**17**	**18**	**19**
Assumption Day *(Roman Catholic)* Independence Day *(India)* National Day *(Liechtenstein)*	Political Restitution Day *(Dominican Republic)*			Independence Day *(Indonesia)* San Martin Day *(Argentina)*	Feast Day of St. Helena *(Russian Orthodox)*	National Aviation Day *(USA)*
20	**21**			**22**	**23**	**24**
Constitution Day *(Hungary)*	Anniversary of the Lincoln-Douglas Debates *(USA)*			Festival of the Immaculate Heart of Mary *(Roman Catholic)*	Liberation Day *(Romania)*	Flag Day *(Liberia)* Feast of St. Bartholomew *(Roman Catholic, Anglican, Lutheran)*
25	**26**	**27**	**28**	**29**	**30**	**31**
Constitution Day *(Paraguay)* Independence Day *(Uruguay)*	Sultan's Birthday *(Zanzibar, Tanzania)* Woman's Equality Day *(USA)*	Lyndon Baines Johnson's Birthday	Johann Wolfgang von Goethe's Birthday	National Uprising Day *(Czechoslovakia)*	Feast Day of St. Rose of Lima *(Peru)*	Malaysia Day *(Malaysia)* Independence Day *(Trinidad and Tobago)*

SEPTEMBER

Movable Days

Labor Day (*USA*)
Rosh Hashanah*
(*Jewish*)
Fisherman's Walk Day
(*Scotland*)
Yom Kippur* (*Jewish*)

Confucian Festival
(*Korea*)
Choosuk, or Moon
Festival (*Korea*)

*or October

1	2	3	4	5	6	7
Revolution Day (*Libya*) Heroes' Day (*Tanzania*)	Independence Day (*Vietnam*)	Independence Day (*Qatar*)	Founding of Los Angeles (*USA*)	First meeting of the Continental Congress (*USA*)	Somhlolo Day (*Swaziland*) Defense Day (*Pakistan*)	Independence Day (*Brazil*) Granddad's Day (*USA*)
8	**9**	**10**	**11**			**12**
National Day (*Andorra*) Independence Day (*Guinea, Bissau*) Republic Day (*Uganda*) World Literary Day	Leo Tolstoy's Birthday Liberation or Freedom Day (*Bulgaria*)	National Day (*Belize*)	D. H. Lawrence's Birthday			Respect for the Aged Day (*Japan*)
13	**14**	**15**	**16**			**17**
Anniversary of the Battle of Quebec (*Canada*)	Anniversary of the death of Dante Alighieri (*Italy*)	Independence Day (*Costa Rica, El Salvador, Guatemala, Honduras, Nicaragua*)	Independence Day (*Singapore*)			Citizenship Day (*USA*)
18		**19**	**20**	**21**	**22**	**23**
Independence Day (*Chile*) Samuel Johnson's Birthday		Feast Day of St. Januarius (*Roman Catholic*)	Founding of Equal Rights Party (*USA*) Fall Equinox	Independence Day (*Malta*) H. G. Wells's Birthday	Independence Day (*Mali*)	Unification Day (*Saudi Arabia*)
24	**25**	**26**	**27**	**28**	**29**	**30**
Feast of Nuestra Senora de las Mercedes (*Dominican Republic and Peru*)	Government Day (*Rwanda*)	George Gershwin's Birthday Beginning of Two-Day Ceremony of the Dead (*Cambodia*)	Sandor Kisfaludy's Birthday	Fiesta of San Miguel (*Mexico*) Confucius' Birthday	Michaelmas Day (*Roman Catholic*) Constitution Day (*Borneo*)	Independence Day (*Botswana*)

OCTOBER

Movable Days

Husain Day
 (*Shiite Islamic*)
Festival of the
 Emperor Gods
 (*Penang, Malaysia*)

Paung-daw-U Festival
 (*Burma*)

1	2	3	4	5	6	7
Unification Day (*Cameroon*) Independence Day (*Nigeria*) Armed Forces Day (*South Korea*)	Mahatma Gandhi's Birthday	National Foundation Day (*South Korea*) Leyden Day (*The Netherlands*)	Independence Day (*Lesotho*) Feast Day of St. Francis (*Italy*)	Republic Day (*Portugal*) Army Day (*Indonesia*)	Universal Children's Day	Constitution Day (*East Germany*)
8	**9**	**10**	**11**	**12**	**13**	**14**
Feast Day of St. Bridget (*Sweden*)	Feast Day of St. Denis (*France*) Day of National Dignity (*Peru*) Independence Day (*Uganda*)	Alexis Kivi Day (*Finland*)	Revolution Day (*Panama*)	Columbus Day (*USA*) Independence Day (*Equatorial Guinea*)	Feast Day of St. Edward (*Great Britain*)	Yemen National Day
15	**16**	**17**	**18**	**19**	**20**	**21**
Virgil's Birthday World Poetry Day	National Heroes' Day (*Jamaica*) Eugene O'Neill's Birthday	Black Poetry Day (*USA*) Dessalines Day (*Haiti*) Mother's Day (*Malawi*)	Feast Day of St. Luke (*Roman Catholic, Christian, Lutheran*)	Feast Day of St. Peter (*Roman Catholic*)	Revolution Day (*Guatemala*) Kenyatta Day (*Kenya*)	Army Day (*Honduras*) Revolution Day (*Sudan*)
22	**23**	**24**	**25**		**26**
Veterans Day (*Puerto Rico*) Jidai Matsuri or Festival of Eras (*Japan*)	Chulalongkorn Day (*Thailand*)	United Nations Day Independence Day (*Zambia*) Anton van Leeuwen-hoek's Birthday	Pablo Picasso's Birthday Thanksgiving Day (*Virgin Islands*)	International Red Cross Day Feast Day of St. Demetrios (*Greece*)
27	**28**	**29**	**30**		**31**
Cuba Discovery Day (*Cuba*) Dylan Thomas's Birthday	Foundation of the Republic Day (*Czechoslovakia*) Ochi Day (*Greece*)	James Boswell's Birthday Republic Days (*Turkey*)	John Adams's Birthday		Halloween or All Hallows' Eve (*USA*) UNICEF Day

NOVEMBER

1	2	3	4	5	6	7
All Saints' Day *(Christian)* Revolution Day *(Algeria)* Memorial Day *(Toga)*	All Souls' Day *(Christian)* Dia de Muertos, Day of the Dead *(Mexico)* Dia de Finados, Day of the Dead *(Portugal)*	Culture Day *(Japan)* Independence Day *(Panama)*	Flag Day *(Panama)* Feast Day of St. Charles *(Roman Catholic)*	Guy Fawkes Day *(Great Britain)*	Gustavus Adolphus Day *(Sweden)*	Albert Camus's Birthday

8	9		10	11	12	13
Feast of St. Claude, sculptors' patron saint *(Christian)*	Tree Festival Day *(Tunisia)*		Hero and Youth Day *(Indonesia)* Anniversary of the death of Imam Ali *(Iran)*	Armistice Day *(USA, Belgium, France)* Feodor Dostoyevsky's Birthday	Republic Day *(Austria)* Remembrance Day *(Bermuda)*	Robert Louis Stevenson's Birthday

14	15	16	17	18	19	20
Claude Monet's Birthday	Feast Day of St. Albertus Magnus *(Roman Catholic)* Proclamation of the Republic Day *(Brazil)*	William C. Handy's Birthday	Army Day *(Zaire)*	Army Day *(Haiti)*	Prince Rainier III's Birthday *(Monaco)*	Revolution Day *(Mexico)*

21	22	23	24			25
Voltaire's Birthday	George Eliot's Birthday	Labor Thanksgiving Day *(Japan)*	Anniversary of the Second Republic *(Zaire)*			Feast of St. Catherine of Alexandria *(France)*

26	27	28	29			30
Independence Day *(Lebanon)*	Robert R. Livingston's Birthday	Independence Day *(Albania)* Republic Day *(Burundi)* Republic Day *(Chad)* Independence Day *(Mauritania)*	Liberation Day *(Albania)* Proclamation of the Republic Days *(Yugoslavia)*			Independence Day *(Barbados)* Bonifacio Day or National Heroes' Day *(Philippines)*

DECEMBER

Movable Days

Hanukkah *(Jewish)*
Advent
Guru Tegh Bahadur's
 Martyrdom Day
 (Sikh)

1	2		3	4	5
National Day *(African Republic)* Mocidade Day *(Portugal)*	Pan American Health Day		Birthday of Joseph Conrad Feast Day of St. Francis Xavier *(Borneo, Australia, China)*	Day of the Artisans *(Mexico)*	Discovery Day *(Haiti)* Constitution Day *(USSR)* St. Nicholas' Eve *(Europe)*
6	**7**		**8**	**9**	**10**
Feast Day of St. Nicholas *(USSR and Europe)* Independence Day *(Finland)*	Day of National Mourning *(Cuba)*		Mother's Day *(Spain)* Feast of the Immaculate Conception *(Roman Catholic)*	Independence Day *(Tanzania)*	Human Rights Day Constitution Day *(Thailand)*
11	**12**	**13**	**14**	**15**	**16**	**17**
Scaling Day *(Switzerland)* Republic Day *(Upper Volta)*	Fiesta of Our Lady of Guadalupe *(Mexico)* Day of the Indians *(El Salvador)*	Lucia Day *(Sweden)*	Feast Day of St. Spyridon *(Greece)* Anniversary of the death of Imam Ja'far Sadeg *(Iran)*	Kingdom Day or Statute Day *(The Netherlands)*	Jane Austen's Birthday Ludwig van Beethoven's Birthday Victory Day *(Bangladesh)*	Independence Day *(Colombia)*
18	**19**	**20**	**21**	**22**	**23**	**24**
The Fiesta of the Virgin of the Lonely *(Mexico)* Republic Day *(Niger)*	Princess Bernice Pauahi Bishop's Birthday *(Hawaii, USA)*	Anniversary of acquisition of Louisiana Territory *(USA)* Winter Solstice	Joseph Stalin's Birthday	International Arbor Day	John Canoe Day *(Jamaica)*	Independence Day *(Libya)* Christmas Eve *(Christian)*
25	**26**	**27**	**28**	**29**	**30**	**31**
Christmas Day *(Christian)* Constitution Day *(Taiwan)*	Mao Tse-tung's Birthday Feast Day of St. Stephen *(Hungary)* Boxing Day *(Great Britain)*	Feast of St. John the Evangelist *(Scandinavia)*	Feast of the Holy Innocents *(Christian)* Woodrow Wilson's Birthday	Pablo Casals's Birthday	Rizal Day *(Philippines)* Rudyard Kipling's Birthday	New Year's Eve or Watch Night

LUNAR CALENDAR

1981

DATE		MOON PHASE	TIME
JAN.	6	N	7:25 A
	13	Q	10:11 A
	20	F	7:40 A
	28	W	4:20 A
FEB.	4	N	10:15 P
	11	Q	5:50 P
	18	F	10:59 P
	27	W	1:15 A
MAR.	6	N	10:32 A
	13	Q	1:51 A
	20	F	3:23 P
	28	W	7:35 P
APR.	4	N	8:20 P
	11	Q	11:11 A
	19	F	8:00 A
	27	W	10:16 A
MAY	4	N	4:20 A
	10	Q	10:23 P
	19	F	0:05 A
	26	W	9:01 P
JUN.	2	N	11:32 A
	9	Q	11:34 A
	17	F	3:05 P
	25	W	4:26 A
JUL.	1	N	7:04 P
	9	Q	2:40 A
	17	F	4:40 A
	24	W	9:41 A
	31	N	3:53 A
AUG.	7	Q	7:27 P
	15	F	4:38 P
	22	W	2:17 P
	29	N	2:45 P
SEP.	6	Q	1:27 P
	14	F	3:10 A
	20	W	7:48 P
	28	N	4:08 A
OCT.	6	Q	7:46 A
	13	F	0:50 P
	20	W	3:42 A
	27	N	8:15 P
NOV.	5	Q	1:10 A
	11	F	10:28 P
	18	W	2:55 P
	26	N	2:40 P
DEC.	4	Q	4:23 P
	11	F	8:42 A
	18	W	5:48 A
	26	N	10:11 A

1982

DATE		MOON PHASE	TIME
JAN.	3	Q	4:47 A
	9	F	7:54 P
	16	W	11:59 P
	25	N	4:57 A
FEB.	1	Q	2:29 P
	8	F	7:58 P
	15	W	8:22 P
	23	N	9:14 P
MAR.	2	Q	10:16 P
	9	F	8:46 P
	17	W	5:16 P
	25	N	10:19 A
APR.	1	Q	5:09 A
	8	F	10:19 A
	16	W	0:43 P
	23	N	8:30 P
	30	Q	0:08 P
MAY	8	F	0:46 A
	16	W	5:12 A
	23	N	4:41 A
	29	Q	8:07 P
JUN.	6	F	4:00 P
	14	W	6:07 P
	21	N	11:53 A
	28	Q	5:57 A
JUL.	6	F	7:33 A
	14	W	3:48 A
	20	N	6:58 P
	27	Q	6:23 P
AUG.	4	F	10:35 P
	12	W	11:09 A
	19	N	2:46 A
	26	Q	9:51 A
SEP.	3	F	0:29 P
	10	W	5:20 P
	17	N	0:10 P
	25	Q	4:08 A
OCT.	3	F	1:09 A
	9	W	11:27 P
	17	N	0:05 A
	25	Q	0:09 A
NOV.	1	F	0:58 P
	8	W	6:39 A
	15	N	3:11 P
	23	Q	8:07 P
DEC.	1	F	0:22 A
	7	W	3:54 P
	15	N	9:19 A
	23	Q	2:18 P
	30	F	11:34 A

1983

DATE		MOON PHASE	TIME
JAN.	6	W	4:01 A
	14	N	5:09 A
	22	Q	5:35 A
	28	F	10:27 P
FEB.	4	W	7:18 P
	13	N	0:33 A
	20	Q	5:33 P
	27	F	8:59 A
MAR.	6	W	1:17 P
	14	N	5:44 P
	22	Q	2:26 A
	28	F	7:28 P
APR.	5	W	8:39 A
	13	N	7:59 A
	20	Q	8:59 A
	27	F	6:32 P
MAY	5	W	3:44 A
	12	N	7:26 P
	19	Q	2:18 P
	26	F	6:49 P
JUN.	3	W	9:08 P
	11	N	4:38 P
	17	Q	7:47 P
	25	F	8:33 A
JUL.	3	W	0:13 P
	10	N	0:19 P
	17	Q	2:51 A
	24	F	11:28 P
AUG.	2	W	0:53 A
	8	N	7:19 P
	15	Q	0:48 P
	23	F	3:00 P
	31	W	11:23 A
SEP.	7	N	2:36 A
	14	Q	2:25 A
	21	F	6:37 A
	29	W	8:06 P
OCT.	6	N	11:17 A
	13	Q	7:43 P
	21	F	9:54 P
	29	W	3:38 P
NOV.	4	N	10:22 P
	12	Q	3:50 P
	20	F	0:30 P
	27	W	10:51 A
DEC.	4	N	0:27 P
	12	Q	1:10 P
	20	F	2:01 A
	26	W	6:53 P

1984

DATE		MOON PHASE	TIME
JAN.	3	N	5:17 A
	11	Q	9:49 A
	18	F	2:06 P
	25	W	4:49 A
FEB.	1	N	11:47 P
	10	Q	4:01 P
	17	F	0:42 P
	23	W	5:13 P
MAR.	2	N	6:32 P
	10	Q	6:28 P
	17	F	10:11 A
	24	W	7:59 A
APR.	1	N	0:11 P
	9	Q	4:52 A
	15	F	7:12 P
	23	W	0:27 A
MAY	1	N	3:47 P
	8	Q	11:51 A
	15	F	4:30 A
	22	W	5:46 P
	30	N	4:49 P
JUN.	6	Q	4:42 P
	13	F	2:43 P
	21	W	11:11 A
	29	N	3:19 A
JUL.	5	Q	9:05 P
	13	F	2:21 A
	21	W	4:02 A
	28	N	11:52 A
AUG.	4	Q	2:34 A
	11	F	3:44 P
	19	W	7:42 P
	26	N	7:27 P
SEP.	2	Q	10:31 A
	10	F	7:02 A
	18	W	9:32 A
	25	N	3:12 A
OCT.	1	Q	9:53 P
	9	F	11:59 P
	17	W	9:15 P
	24	N	0:09 P
	31	Q	1:09 P
NOV.	8	F	5:44 P
	16	W	7:00 A
	22	N	10:58 P
	30	Q	8:02 A
DEC.	8	F	10:54 A
	15	W	3:26 P
	22	N	11:48 A
	30	Q	5:29 A

1985

DATE		MOON PHASE	TIME
JAN.	7	F	2:17 A
	13	W	11:28 P
	21	N	2:29 A
	29	Q	3:30 A
FEB.	5	F	3:20 P
	12	W	7:58 A
	19	N	6:44 P
	27	Q	11:42 P
MAR.	7	F	2:14 A
	13	W	5:35 P
	21	N	0:00 P
	29	Q	4:12 A
APR.	5	F	11:33 A
	12	W	4:43 A
	20	N	5:23 A
	28	Q	4:26 A
MAY	4	F	7:54 P
	11	W	5:35 P
	19	N	9:42 P
	27	Q	0:57 P
JUN.	3	F	3:51 A
	10	W	8:20 A
	18	N	11:59 A
	25	Q	6:54 P
JUL.	2	F	0:09 P
	10	W	0:51 A
	17	N	11:57 P
	24	Q	11:40 P
	31	F	9:42 P
AUG.	8	W	6:29 P
	16	N	10:07 A
	23	Q	4:37 A
	30	F	9:28 A
SEP.	7	W	0:17 P
	14	N	7:21 A
	21	Q	11:04 A
	29	F	0:10 A
OCT.	7	W	5:05 A
	14	N	4:34 A
	20	Q	8:14 P
	28	F	5:39 P
NOV.	5	W	8:07 P
	12	N	2:21 P
	19	Q	9:05 A
	27	F	0:43 A
DEC.	5	W	9:02 A
	12	N	0:55 A
	19	Q	1:59 A
	27	F	7:31 A

Q = Quarter Moon   **N** = New Moon
F = Full Moon   **A** = A.M.
W = Waning (Three Quarter) Moon   **P** = P.M.

1986

DATE		MOON PHASE	TIME	
JAN.	3	W	7:48	P
	10	N	0:23	P
	17	Q	10:14	P
	26	F	0:32	A
FEB.	2	W	4:42	A
	9	N	0:56	A
	16	Q	7:56	P
	24	F	3:03	A
MAR.	3	W	0:18	P
	10	N	2:53	P
	18	Q	4:40	P
	26	F	3:03	A
APR.	1	W	7:31	P
	9	N	6:09	A
	17	Q	10:36	A
	24	F	0:47	P
MAY	1	W	3:23	P
	8	N	10:11	P
	17	Q	1:01	A
	23	F	8:46	P
	30	W	0:56	P
JUN.	7	N	2:01	P
	15	Q	0:01	P
	22	F	3:43	A
	29	W	0:54	A
JUL.	7	N	4:56	A
	14	Q	8:11	P
	21	F	10:41	P
	28	W	3:35	P
AUG.	5	N	6:37	P
	13	Q	2:22	A
	19	F	6:55	A
	27	W	8:40	A
SEP.	4	N	7:11	A
	11	Q	7:42	A
	18	F	5:35	A
	26	W	3:19	A
OCT.	3	N	6:56	P
	10	Q	1:29	P
	17	F	7:23	P
	25	W	10:27	P
NOV.	2	N	6:03	A
	8	Q	9:12	P
	16	F	0:13	P
	24	W	4:51	P
DEC.	1	N	4:44	P
	8	Q	8:03	A
	16	F	7:06	A
	24	W	9:18	A
	31	N	3:11	A

1987

DATE		MOON PHASE	TIME	
JAN.	6	Q	10:36	P
	15	F	2:32	A
	22	W	10:46	P
	29	N	1:46	P
FEB.	5	Q	4:22	P
	13	F	8:59	P
	21	W	8:57	A
	28	N	0:52	A
MAR.	7	Q	11:59	A
	15	F	1:14	P
	22	W	4:23	P
	29	N	0:47	P
APR.	6	Q	7:49	A
	14	F	2:32	A
	20	W	10:16	P
	28	N	1:35	A
MAY	6	Q	2:27	A
	13	F	0:51	P
	20	W	4:03	A
	27	N	3:15	P
JUN.	4	Q	6:54	P
	11	F	8:50	P
	18	W	11:04	A
	26	N	5:38	A
JUL.	4	Q	8:35	A
	11	F	3:34	A
	17	W	8:18	P
	25	N	8:39	P
AUG.	2	Q	7:25	P
	9	F	10:18	A
	16	W	8:26	P
	24	N	0:00	P
SEP.	1	Q	3:49	A
	7	F	6:14	P
	14	W	11:46	P
	23	N	3:09	A
	30	Q	10:40	A
OCT.	7	F	4:13	A
	14	W	6:07	P
	22	N	5:29	P
	29	Q	5:11	P
NOV.	5	F	4:47	P
	13	W	2:39	P
	21	N	6:34	A
	28	Q	0:38	A
DEC.	5	F	8:02	A
	13	W	11:42	A
	20	N	6:26	A
	27	Q	10:02	A

1988

DATE		MOON PHASE	TIME	
JAN.	4	F	1:42	A
	12	W	7:05	A
	19	N	5:26	A
	25	Q	9:54	P
FEB.	2	F	8:53	P
	10	W	11:02	P
	17	N	3:55	P
	24	Q	0:16	P
MAR.	3	F	4:02	P
	11	W	10:57	A
	18	N	2:03	A
	25	Q	4:43	A
APR.	2	F	9:22	A
	9	W	7:22	P
	16	N	0:01	A
	23	Q	10:33	P
MAY	1	F	11:42	P
	9	W	1:24	A
	15	N	10:12	P
	23	Q	4:50	P
	31	F	10:54	A
JUN.	7	W	6:23	A
	14	N	9:15	A
	22	Q	10:24	A
	29	F	7:47	P
JUL.	6	W	11:37	A
	13	N	9:54	A
	22	Q	2:15	A
	29	F	3:26	A
AUG.	4	W	6:23	P
	12	N	0:32	P
	20	Q	3:53	P
	27	F	10:57	A
SEP.	3	W	3:51	A
	11	N	4:50	A
	19	Q	3:19	A
	25	F	7:08	P
OCT.	2	W	4:59	P
	10	N	9:50	P
	18	Q	1:02	P
	25	F	4:36	A
NOV.	1	W	10:13	A
	9	N	2:21	P
	16	Q	9:36	P
	23	F	3:54	P
DEC.	1	W	6:51	A
	9	N	5:37	A
	16	Q	5:41	A
	23	F	5:30	A
	31	W	4:58	A

1989

DATE		MOON PHASE	TIME	
JAN.	7	N	7:23	P
	14	Q	1:59	P
	21	F	9:35	P
	30	W	2:03	A
FEB.	6	N	7:38	A
	12	Q	11:16	P
	20	F	3:33	P
	28	W	8:09	P
MAR.	7	N	6:20	P
	14	Q	10:12	A
	22	F	9:59	A
	30	W	10:23	A
APR.	6	N	3:33	A
	12	Q	11:14	P
	21	F	3:14	A
	28	W	8:47	P
MAY	5	N	11:47	A
	12	Q	2:21	P
	20	F	6:17	P
	28	W	4:02	A
JUN.	3	N	7:54	P
	11	Q	7:00	A
	19	F	6:58	A
	26	W	9:10	A
JUL.	3	N	5:00	A
	11	Q	0:20	A
	18	F	5:43	P
	25	W	1:32	P
AUG.	1	N	4:07	P
	9	Q	5:30	P
	17	F	3:08	A
	23	W	6:41	P
	31	N	5:46	A
SEP.	8	Q	9:50	A
	15	F	11:52	A
	22	W	2:11	A
	29	N	9:48	P
OCT.	8	Q	0:53	A
	14	F	8:33	P
	21	W	1:20	P
	29	N	3:28	P
NOV.	6	Q	2:12	P
	13	F	5:52	A
	20	W	4:45	A
	28	N	9:42	A
DEC.	6	Q	1:27	A
	12	F	4:31	P
	19	W	11:56	P
	28	N	3:21	A

1990

DATE		MOON PHASE	TIME	
JAN.	4	Q	10:41	A
	11	F	4:58	A
	18	W	9:18	P
	26	N	7:21	P
FEB.	2	Q	6:33	P
	9	F	7:17	P
	17	W	6:49	P
	25	N	8:55	A
MAR.	4	Q	2:06	P
	11	F	11:00	A
	19	W	2:32	P
	26	N	7:49	P
APR.	2	Q	10:25	A
	10	F	3:20	A
	18	W	7:04	A
	25	N	4:28	A
MAY	1	Q	8:19	P
	9	F	7:32	P
	17	W	7:46	P
	24	N	11:48	A
	31	Q	8:12	P
JUN.	8	F	11:02	A
	16	W	4:49	A
	22	N	6:56	P
	29	Q	10:09	P
JUL.	8	F	1:25	A
	15	W	11:05	A
	22	N	2:55	A
	29	Q	2:03	P
AUG.	6	F	2:21	P
	13	W	3:55	P
	20	N	0:40	P
	28	Q	7:35	A
SEP.	5	F	1:47	A
	11	W	8:54	P
	19	N	0:47	A
	27	Q	2:07	A
OCT.	4	F	0:03	P
	11	W	3:32	A
	18	N	3:38	P
	26	Q	8:28	P
NOV.	2	F	9:49	P
	9	W	1:03	P
	17	N	9:06	A
	25	Q	1:13	P
DEC.	2	F	7:50	A
	9	W	2:05	P
	17	N	4:23	A
	25	Q	3:17	A
	31	F	6:36	P

BIBLIOGRAPHY

Arisian, Khoren. *The New Wedding: Creating Your Own Marriage Ceremony.* New York: Alfred A. Knopf, 1973.

Bachelard, Gaston. *La Flamme d'une Chandelle.* Paris: Presses Universitaires de France, 1961.

Beane, Wendell C. and William G. Doty, eds. *Myths, Rites, and Symbols: A Mircea Eliade Reader.* 2 vols. New York: Harper & Row, 1976.

Beyer, Stephen. *The Cult of Tara: Magic and Ritual in Tibet.* Berkeley: University of California Press, 1973.

Blair, Lawrence. *Rhythms of Vision: The Changing Pattern of Belief.* London: Croon Helm, 1975.

Bord, Janet and Colin Bord. *Mysterious Britain.* Brooklyn, NY: Beekman Publishers, 1978.

Bramly, Serge. *Terre Wakan: Univers Sacre des Indien d'Amerique du Nord.* Paris: R. Laffont, 1974.

Burland, C. A. *Myths of Life & Death.* New York: Crown Publishers, 1974.

Campbell, Joseph. *The Mythic Image.* Princeton, NJ: Princeton University Press, 1975.

Chevalier, Jean and Alain Gheerbrant, eds. *Dictionnaire de Symboles.* Paris: R. Laffont, 1969.

Cirlot, J. E. *A Dictionary of Symbols.* New York: Philosophical Library, 1972.

Covarrubias, Miguel. *Island of Bali.* New York: Alfred A. Knopf, 1937.

Deraul, Akron. *Secret Societies, Yesterday and Today.* London: F. Muller, 1961.

David-Neel, Alexandra. *Magic and Mystery in Tibet.* Secaucus, NJ: University Books, 1958.

Douglas, Nik. *The Book of Matan.* Suffolk, England: Neville Spearman, 1977.

Eliade, Mircea. *Shamanism: Archaic Techniques of Ecstasy.* Translated by Willard R. Trask. New York: Pantheon Books, 1964.

Evans-Wentz, W. Y. *The Tibetan Book of the Dead.* New York: Oxford University Press, 1957.

Gaignebet, Claude and Marie-Claude Florentin. *Le Carnaval: Essais de Mythologie Populaire.* Paris: Payot, 1974.

Gardner, Robert and Karl G. Heider. *Gardens of War: Life and Death in the New Guinea Stone Age.* New York: Random House, 1969.

Fergusson, Erna. *Dancing Gods: Indian Ceremonials of New Mexico and Arizona.* New York: Alfred A. Knopf, 1931.

Huber, Leonard. *New Orleans: A Pictorial History.* New York: Crown Publishers, 1971.

Hutchison, Ruth and Ruth Adams. *Every Day's a Holiday.* New York: Harper & Row, 1951.

James, E. O. *Origins of Sacrifice: A Study in Comparative Religion.* London: J. Murray, 1933.

Jung, Carl G. *Man and His Symbols.* Garden City, NY: Doubleday, 1964.

Koestler, Arthur. *The Roots of Coincidence.* London: Hutchinson & Co. Ltd., 1972.

Krythe, Maymie R. *All About American Holidays.* New York: Harper & Row, 1962.

LaChapelle, Dolores and Janet Bourgue. *Celebrations for Everyone Young and Old.* Silverton, CO: Finn Hill Arts, 1976.

Lauret, Jean-Claude. *Les Fetes a travers la France.* Paris: Balland, 1972.

Leach, Maria, ed. *Standard Dictionary of Folklore, Mythology and Legend.* 2 vols. New York: Funk & Wagnalls, 1972.

Lommel, Andreas. *Shamanism: The Beginnings of Art.* Translated by Michael Bullock. New York: McGraw-Hill, 1967.

Marciceau, Jacques. *Historie des Rites Sexuals.* Paris: R. Laffont, 1971.

Michell, John F. *The Earth Spirit: Its Ways, Shrines and Mysteries.* London: Thames and Hudson, 1975.

Myers, Robert J. and Hallmark Cards eds. *Celebrations: The Complete Book of American Holidays.* New York: Doubleday, 1972.

Neumann, Erich. *The Great Mother: An Analysis of the Archtype.* Translated by Ralph Monheim. Princeton, NJ: Princeton University Press, 1970.

New Larousse Encyclopedia of Mythology. London: Hamlyn, 1968.

Price, Christine. *Happy Days.* New York: U.S. Committee UNICEF, 1979.

Purce, Jill. *The Mystic Spiral: Journey of the Soul.* London: Thames and Hudson, 1975.

Purdy, Susan Gold. *Festivals for You to Celebrate.* Philadelphia, PA: Lippincott, 1969.

Scherer, Joanna Cohan. *Indians: The Camera Reveals the Reality of North American Indian Life, 1847–1928.* New York: Crown Publishers, 1974.

Strassfield, Michael. *The Jewish Catalog: A Do-It-Yourself Kit.* Philadelphia, PA: Jewish Publications, 1973.

Sykes, Homer. *Once a Year: Some Traditional British Customs.* London: G. Fraser, 1977.

Tanaka, Seno. *The Tea Ceremony.* New York: Harmony Books, 1977.

Verroust, Jacques and Michel Parent. *Fetes en France.* Paris: Vander, 1971.

Villas Boas, Claudio and Orlando Villas Boas. *Xingu: The Indians, Their Myths.* Edited by Kenneth S. Brecher. Translated by Susanna Hertelendy Rudge. New York: Farrar, Straus & Giroux, 1973.

Weiner, Herbert. *9½ Mystics: The Kabbala Today.* New York: Holt, Rinehart & Winston, 1969.

Williams, John Alden, ed. *Great Religions of Modern Man.* 6 vols. New York: George Brazillier, 1962.

ACKNOWLEDGMENTS

For Elohim and all the good spirits and muses—Matuta, Nut, Vega, Ganesh, Saraswati, Lakshmi, Kali, Iemanja, Pombajira, Oxosi, La Guadelupe, San Sebastian, Erzuli, Fatima, Sanghyang Widi and many more—who have inspired, guided, and protected me during my visual and verbal peregrinations.

In appreciation of tradition and of the communities that perpetrate rural and urban feasts. In deference to the irreverent leprechauns who chew gum during anthropological dramas. In recognition of the anguish of separation that nurtures our culture. To the instinct of survival—it jolts me, keeps me searching back, projects me forward, and leaves me stationary. In memory and anticipation of all the small and large gatherings, of the moment when fear is surpassed and relief is in sight.

I offer my gratitude to all the people represented in this book and to the ones who are not, but who have helped uncondi- tionally, some of whom are listed in the following credits:

To
My family, ever present and loving, including Mati Papati.

The harmonious team of Bruce Harris, whose unfailing interest and counsel throughout the progress of this book made possible its intricate realization, and Manuela Soares, whose editorial skill efficiently supervised the completion of every detail.

The many refinements, research, and rekindled celebrations of Carol Tannenhauser.

The strong and delicate designs of Joan Peckolick.

Barbara and Stanley Mortimer for keeping the country roads open.

Jocelyne the Zen survivor.

Elianne, Jean Pierre, and Stephanie Laffont whose eyes click smiling.

The Sygma Photo News Agency.

Harry, Gigi, Wendy, and Tessa Benson for their enthusiasm.

Phil Pesoni at Lexington Lab who valiantly walked his pierced body back to the darkroom.

D. L. Hopper, who shattered my innocence and encouraged me to take all my own photos.

Christiane Dickinson's thoughtful motions.

Liz Weiner's subterranean gallery.

Lorraine Pinto and her sculpted dreams in Mexico City.

Colette and Peter.

Stella and Stuart.

Kao in Rio, imperturbable open heart and *corpo fechado*.

Julio Bandeira's stubborn devotion and poetic pedaling and his grandmother and Marie Alice.

Suzie Bentolila's energetic efficiency.

The Rabat Hilton's comfort and its garden full of rosemary bushes.

Tayeb Sadiki's delightful Islamic hand, and the two other rascals.

The Youness family in Cairo who scooped us up from the cold and put us in Nadia's room.

The Swedish embassy on the Nile.

The Tel Aviv Hilton's yummy delicatessen and superfast telephone operator to New York and the balcony with the view of the sunrise on the Sea of Galilee.

Ching Ho Cheng.

Bubbles, the Maharajah of Jaipur, who turned the Rajmahal palace lawn into a spectrum splash.

Ayesha, the Maharanee of Jaipur, who dislikes ceremonies but presides over them beautifully.

Chota Chudasama kindly from India.

Ram Kholi, who travels creatively.

Allan Fernandez and Rabindra Seth at the India Tourism Development Corporation.

The restful Maurya Hotel and the kind help of I.T.C.

Wendy Stark's ever-positive spirit.

The Soaltee Hotel's owner in Kathmandu, whose help was invaluable.

Tom and Julie Britt, Willy and Robert, hoping for their safety.

Richard Avedon.

The most gracious staff of the Hyatt Rama in busy Bangkok and the Bonnard family.

Wija and Tati Waworuntu of Tandjung Sari Hotel in Sanur, Bali, who remain as hospitable and generous as ever despite a decade of ever-increasing prosperity.

Lawrence Blair, whose rhythms of visions gently unfurl above the rice fields.

Lorne Blair, whose persevering sight goes further.

The Pury, purveyor of many a story, and the music in the beautiful lobby of the Bali Hyatt hotel.

Mr. Kase and Kimura, who displayed the best of Japanese hospitality.

Tim Leary.

The Hyatt Hotel in San Francisco's Union Square and its panoramic view of the city.

Wynn and Sally Chamberlain and the twins, with their inner fire.

Mysterious Steven Marshank, who always wheels in at the right moment.

Jerry Schatzberg.

Maureen Lambray.

Christina Bellin, who loves a good celebration every day.

Helen Studley, who holds the wings at Madison Avenue Travel.

Jerry Ross, a gourmand of life's honey and a dedicated helper.

Marit and Sandy Lieberson in London, who for so many years have made their house my home.

Nicky Haskell's high voltage.

Professor Blau at Columbia University.

Tom Keyes's dissertation.

Carol Thompson.

John Lombardi.

Suzanne Fenn.

Ralph Gibson's clear sight.

Earle Mack's supportive friendship.

Patrick Firpo and hard-working, sweet Claudia Katayanagi.

Inigo de la Huerta and Ignacio, Duque de Segorbe, and their historical lessons on the patio of Casa de Pilato, Sevilla.

Joseph Berger and his family.

Carol and Shelley Gordon.

Frederick Cushing.

Jane Fredericks.

Elie and Francis Ford Coppola.

And to many, so many more people...thank you.